# Tributes to Canon Bill Vanstone
# and *Hebridean Odysseys*

"As my three young sons were growing up in Yorkshire, I started a local group with three other dads, which we called 'Dads and Lads'. Emulating, albeit modestly, the 'Vanstonian' Hebridean trips, we organised 'primitive' camps and (even more primitive) bunk barn trips in the Dales and the Lake District. That was more than 15 years ago. We have expanded our trips to Europe in recent years, adding sailing and skiing to the outdoor skills. The group is still as strong as ever, with annual trips, as the 'lads' now approach their thirties. I've no doubt that the seed for that group, now numbering around 30 people, came from those early Hebridean camps. I also have no doubt that Bill Vanstone had a hugely beneficial impact on my life and on the lives of many, many others."

**Tony Layton editor of *Hebridean Odysseys***

"I was a non-camper who waved them all off and waved them back on their safe return. When returning from the last Colonsay camp, Bill said to me, 'Sarah, standing on Kiloran Bay is the closest I shall ever be to Paradise.'"

**Sarah Samuels (wife of Canon Samuels)**

"Bill's accounts of the camps led me and my family to find out more about these amazing islands. After visiting Colonsay, we were so delighted that, from then on, not only did we tour the Western Isles as a family but I also began to lead camps all over the Hebrides, Orkneys and Shetland. I've now visited some 80 islands over the years (out of a total of around 120). How grateful we all are to Bill Vanstone for having introduced us to these beautiful places, and also for keeping such fascinating accounts of the camps. One can almost smell the *machir* in his writings and hear his chuckles about the things boys said or did. And how grateful we are to Tony for helping to preserve these precious memories of the past."

**Canon Chris Samuels (Bill Vanstone's curate from 1967–1972)**


"Without our Hebridean exploits, I doubt I'd have spent most of my summers working in the Lake District, and I wouldn't have even contemplated a Land's End to John O'Groats walk, which I did a few years later. Bill's academic brilliance was also influential on us. I once called at the vicarage to borrow a football and was met with this: 'So you're not learning any foreign languages, Ian? Learn one!' he ordered. I subsequently took an arts and science degree. My second language is German."

**Ian Aitchison**

"I attended four of my uncle's camps in the 1950s and 1960s. I was an outsider from Leeds on holiday in wild and distant places, but I was embedded for a while within a Kirkholt community. I remember the way Uncle Bill would tilt his head, fix his gaze on you, and then deliver some wry and perceptive observation. His questioning of values helped me think independently."

**Richard Vanstone (nephew of Canon Vanstone)**

"A great highlight of each of my years from the age of 8 to 18 were the camps led by Bill. It wasn't just the adventure – sometimes pretty exotic for us Kirkholt boys – nor even having great fun with friends, it was also the opportunity to spend more time with, and learn from, Bill himself. Over my first 20 odd years, Bill was initially 'our vicar', then mentor and, ultimately, friend. The privilege of knowing Bill has been one of the most important influences in my life. Rereading these journals brings back wonderful memories of those adventures as well as his remarkable influence on us all."

**Michael Daman**

# Hebridean Odysseys

Written by Canon WH Vanstone
Edited by Tony Layton

First published 2022 by Compass-Publishing UK

ISBN 978-1-907308-93-2
Copyright © Tony Layton

Edited and typeset by The Book Refinery Ltd
www.thebookrefinery.com

Cover photo © Almay
Back cover inside photo courtesy of Getty Images © Getty Images

For permission requests, contact Tony Layton by phone on 07721 620526, by email at: tony.layton@wordsandpics.co.uk or in writing to Tony Layton, The Paddock, The Street, Addingham LS29 0JY.

A CIP catalogue record for this book is available from the British Library.

Printed and bound by CMP, Poole, Dorset, UK.

*A note on the cover photo:* Highland cattle paddle in front of Breachacha Castle on the Isle of Coll in the Inner Hebrides, one of the many western islands visited in *Hebridean Odysseys.*

*Dedicated to the fortunate 'colleagues' of Bill Vanstone who went 'Round Many Western Isles' during a number of camps in the late 1960s and early 1970s.*

# Contents

# Foreword

## By Tony Layton

Part 1 of *Hebridean Odysseys*, 'What Shall My West Hurt Me?', comprises a series of journals written by Canon WH (Bill) Vanstone[i] – we knew him simply as 'Sir' – which tell the story of six camps of Scouts and Sigma[ii] based at St Thomas' Church in Kirkholt, a council estate in the northern mill town of Rochdale. (See photos on page 90.) These camps, as covered in Part 1, took place from 1968 to 1970. By then, Canon Vanstone had already led a number of boys' camps, going back to the mid-1950s, while serving as a Church of England vicar in two Lancashire council estates – one in Halliwell, Bolton, and the other in Rochdale.

The previous journals also written by Vanstone, not published here, include the following: *So Far So Good*, which tells the story of camps from 1956 to 1963; *A Scilly Diary* (1964); *The Connemara Story* (1965); *Western Extremities* (1966); and *Ghosts Remember in December* (1967).

'What Shall My West Hurt Me?' looks back on what followed, during that series of late 1960s' camps to the Isle of Islay, the Isles of Scilly, the Isle of Coll, Rhoscolyn (on Anglesey, Wales), Galloway and the mid-west of Scotland (including the Isle of Eigg).

---

i. Canon William Hubert Vanstone was born in Mossley, Lancashire, on 9th May 1923, and he died in Cirencester, Gloucestershire, on 4th March 1999.

ii. Sigma – a youth club for older boys at St Thomas' Church, Kirkholt – was formed by Canon WH Vanstone in the late 1960s as a replacement for the local Scout troop (following a difference of viewpoint with the leaders of the local Scout movement). Instead of learning how to rub twigs together to light fires, Sigma helped young teenagers from Kirkholt, a council estate in Rochdale, to thrive in areas of their own choosing. Sigma subsequently became a kind of Hebridean Appreciation Society for those scores of boys (now all men in advanced middle age) who joined in these adventures and benefitted from them in ways they could never have imagined.

Meanwhile, Part 2 of this book, 'Round Many Western Isles', focuses entirely on the Western Isles of Scotland, covering three camps: the first in 1971 (a tour of the Isle of Coll, Barra, North and South Uist, Benbecula, and the Isle of Skye), the second in 1972 (the Isles of Eigg and Canna) and the final camp in this journal in 1973 (the Isle of Colonsay).

There was only one further camp – on the Isle of Gigha – in August 1975, which Canon Vanstone led but failed to record. By then, most of the young men who'd been on the many earlier camps were either (far) away at university or had started work. Bill's health, meanwhile, had started to deteriorate, and he retired from active parish work the following year. A heart attack in 1978 finally persuaded Canon Vanstone to retire fully, and he became an emeritus canon residentiary at Chester Cathedral where, for the following decade, he dedicated himself to serious theological writing. One of his books, *Love's Endeavour, Love's Expense,*[1] won the Collins Biennial Religious Book Award in 1979.

Back in those camping days, however, we young teenagers had no idea of Sir's academic brilliance. He pretty much kept to himself the fact that, more than 20 years before, he had taken a double first-class degree at Balliol College, Oxford, and a starred first-class degree at Cambridge, following active service in the Royal Air Force during the war. Vanstone achieved further distinction in New York, where he studied under the existentialist philosophers Paul Tillich and James Muilenburg at the General Theological Seminary. To be honest, we were more interested in what was for breakfast on camp days – it was usually porridge – rather than Sir's view on the 'Response of being to the love of God'. We were more bemused by his love of single malts, especially Glenfarclas 105, drunk while smoking a Capstan (full strength), rather than any of his intellectual doubts or the mysteries of existence.

We knew Sir was brainy, but we had no idea how much. In an obituary in March 1999, however, *The Independent* described Bill Vanstone as "the most intellectually brilliant of the many able men who were ordained after the Second World War."[2] Back in the late

1960s and early 1970s, we preferred hearing spooky ghost stories from him, as gale-force winds lashed at our tents in that field behind the Coll Hotel on the Isle of Coll, or we'd rather opt for splashing Sir in lovely Atlantic waters by immaculate Isle of Colonsay beaches that went on for ever, or playing endless games of cricket on *machir*[iii] grass by the side of our tents, where we delighted in bowling him out just for a few runs. He was, to be honest, a fairly decent batsman and an even better rugby player. In his late teens, Bill, a sprightly number 9, had impressed many with spectacularly long spin passes from the base of the scrum while playing for the First XV at Bradford Grammar School. But it was his retentive and analytical mind that impressed most. As well as being brilliant at selecting idyllic camp sites in the Hebrides, with views that people today would 'die for', Vanstone had an unusual grasp of philosophy and modern historical methodology – something that made many Oxbridge colleges keen to hire him. Despite all their offers, Vanstone was determined to become and remain a parish clergyman, but one with a difference. The difference he made in the lives of us boys, in our lives then and afterwards, was as wide as the Sound of Mull. He never took a holiday, apart from camping with 'us lot'. We all have much to thank him for.

The journals were originally typed by Vanstone himself – who knows how he found the time in an incredibly busy schedule of caring and preaching? And now, more than a half-century on, I'm guessing there are just a few copies of these journals left, some stowed away in lofts or garages, most falling apart. I kept mine in a chest, and after a life in editing and corporate communications, I decided to pull together two of Vanstone's surviving journals and combine them into this book, which I've called *Hebridean Odysseys*: the stories of nine camps that changed our lives.

I hope you too can see, through these camp stories, just how Canon Vanstone directed an enormous amount of traffic of love and care for those he called his 'colleagues' rather than his 'charges'.

---

iii. *Machir*, or *machair*, is a swathe of soft, grassy land, which is normally found adjacent to coastlines in the Inner and Outer Hebrides. Flat *machir* makes for ideal campsite terrain.

# Introduction

As the places and camps visited in *Hebridean Odysseys* here reveal, our group followed a long-held bias towards the west. It's a bias that seemed to begin as an accident, to continue as a habit, and later, to become established as a tradition.

Some of us have come to detect and appreciate the particular *atmosphere* of the west of Britain, especially of the islands and promontories of the west. Hard though it is to describe, there certainly *is* such an atmosphere. As the focus of British enterprise and prosperity has moved increasingly to the south-east, the west has become – more and more – the land from which people, particularly young people, have left. To those who remain, the west is the place where life has passed them by, the place from which the young and enterprising have departed, and the place whose quietness contains a touch of sadness. For those who have left the west, they've been haunted by the memory of the land of childhood and long ago. For Britons, the west is the 'land of the sunset', and the land of affectionate longing and gentle regret.

It's interesting to reflect that, to Americans, the West means the exact opposite. Their West has been the place of the future, the place of opportunity. Their young people have travelled *to*, not *from*, the West, and their most westerly territories in California are the places where everything is up and coming, new and brash. How very different from the west of Britain. It would be interesting to work out how this difference is reflected in American and British literature.

There's one complication, however. Britain is a part of Europe, and Europeans, from the Greeks onwards, have handed down legends of certain wonderful islands in the western sea – islands of perfect happiness and everlasting youth. The Greeks called them 'The

Hesperides', and they located them somewhere to the west of the Pillars of Hercules (the Straits of Gibraltar), the limit of the world they knew. The Celts called them 'Tir nan Og', the 'Isles of Youth'. So, to the Briton, influenced by European tradition, the west isn't only the land of sunset, and sadness, it's also the hoped-for land of happiness that lies beyond the sunset. Alfred Tennyson put these words into the mouth of a brave old man:

> ...*for my purpose holds*
> *To sail beyond the sunset, and the baths*
> *Of all the western stars, until I die.*
> *It may be that the gulfs will wash us down:*
> *It may be we shall touch the Happy Isles...*[3]

Two centuries earlier, John Donne – writing in sickness and likening his approaching death to a perilous voyage to the west – continues, nonetheless, cheerfully:

> *I joy that, in these straits, I see my west;*
> *For, though their currents yield return to none*
> *What shall my west hurt me? As west and east*
> *In all flat maps (and I am one) are one,*
> *So death doth touch the resurrection*[4]

To these English poets, to travel to the west means to travel bravely, through loss and sadness, to a final happiness. Something of the same thought occurs in John Buchan's strange novel *A Prince of the Captivity*.[5] The brave and generous life of its hero, Adam Melfort, is haunted and inspired by a recurring dream in which he is always trying, but failing, to reach the western shore of a Hebridean island, dimly remembered from his childhood. He dreams it for the last time as he is about to risk and lose his life to save some friends. And this time, in his dream, he doesn't fail, but he comes at last to his western shore and his final contentment.

John Keats continued that theme of fascination for the west in 'On First Looking into Chapman's Homer':

*Much have I travell'd in the realms of gold*
*And many goodly states and kingdoms seen;*
*Round many Western Islands have I been...*[6]

To visit the Hebrides is, indeed, to visit a different world – a realm of gold. Recently, Father Callum McNeill, the parish priest of Eriskay in the Outer Hebrides (population 143) was on the radio, contrasting the life in the "realms of gold" with city life. He said, "In the cities of today – including Tokyo, San Francisco, London and even Glasgow – there's a kind of *hybrid mind* to which nobody assents, but to which everyone defers."[7] But when we visit the Hebrides, and indeed other western islands, we're impressed by a contrast to that "hybrid mind". There's a genuineness in people's opinions, an assurance in their values, and a consistency between what they say about life and how they live it.

Father McNeill is convinced the values and attitudes of the islanders are strong enough to survive, irrespective of the social and economic changes the coming years may bring. Already, change is on the way. Already, a difference has appeared between those islands that are served by a 'drive on, drive off' ferry, and those whose lifeline is the *Loch Arkaig* or the *Claymore*. Already, the prosperity that tourism brings – so remarkably absent from the Isles of Eigg, Colonsay and Canna – appears, ever more, on Islay, Mull and Skye. At the same time, there continues the drift of the population away from the less prosperous islands, including not only Eigg and Colonsay but also Coll and Tiree. This drift has gone on for many years, but now, it seems to me that it's no longer accepted simply with sadness and resignation by those who stay.

Father McNeill believes the stability and tranquillity of the Hebridean character has less to do with the physical *peace* in which Hebrideans live, and rather more with the physical *endurance* to which life obliges them. It seems that the physical buffeting by wind, rain and storm, and the experience of being cold, hungry or wet creates in them – indeed, in man – a deep inner serenity. This is an interesting thought: I've often observed at camp what a beneficial effect a wet or stormy day can have on our spirits, our comradeship and our willingness to help one another. Bad weather on camp doesn't make us ill-tempered, rather the reverse. It's in the sunshine when hints of bad temper sometimes arise. It may be that man is designed for a habitat that brings him, from time to time, the experience of physical hardship, a need for endurance. And when in such a place, perhaps man shows himself at his best? If this is so, it's a justification – if one were needed – for camping, and especially for the *lightweight* and even *primitive* camping that has always been our custom.

Perhaps these reflections aren't wholly out of place in a little book about camping. For a camp will be enjoyed by no one who isn't prepared to take a few roughs with the smooth. Indeed, the best and most memorable moments of a camp are generally those when a way has been found through some forbidding difficulty of weather or circumstance.

I count myself fortunate to have had such good and companionable colleagues on the camps recorded here. I say 'colleagues' rather than 'charges' because the maturing of charges into colleagues has been one of the best features of all our camping adventures. Shared experience soon overcomes the disparities of age. For much of the enjoyment, I've been indebted to eyes keener than my own in noticing things, to hands more competent than mine in doing things, and to wit sharper than my own in commenting on events in ways more perceptive, and amusing, than I ever could. The company in which I've been 'round many Western Isles' has had much to do with making them my own "realms of gold".

For that company, as well as for the solace of my own declining years, I've written this book. I hope that, despite its incompleteness and imperfections, it will afford a little enjoyment. If it doesn't, please don't throw it away. Put it somewhere safe until you're old and grey and full of years – that's to say about 25 or so. Then read it again, and I think you'll enjoy it, not because of its style or descriptions or anything like that, but because it will remind you of what you did and what you shared back in the old days. Those old days when you could still have a golden beach entirely to yourself on a summer afternoon, and when you could still gather driftwood for cooking. When, for a few days, your biggest worry was what to buy as a present for your mum and dad.

*William Hubert Vanstone*
*Kirkholt, Rochdale, 1971*

# PART 1

What Shall My West Hurt Me?

# Chapter 1

## The Isle of Islay, June 1968

In June 1967, standing on a hilltop above Glen Ross in the Isle of Arran, a few of us saw, away to the west, what we took to be the hills of Islay, and with the song of 'Islay Westering Home' much in our minds at that time (as the song had been the finale in our most recent gang show), Michael Daman and I made a resolution that – one day, in the not too distant future – we'd sail to Islay.

It was fortunate that we proceeded with our resolution the following year, for soon afterwards, the boat service between Gourock and East Tarbert was abolished, and the journey westwards to Islay must have lost half of its curious and leisurely charm. But in 1968, it was still possible, after an overnight journey to Glasgow, to catch the busy little steamer at Gourock at about 10am and to weave one's way across the River Clyde, through the narrow water of the Kyles of Bute, and up the lower reaches of Loch Fyne to East Tarbert, calling on the way to pick up the odd passenger or deposit the odd parcel at the little quays of Innellan, Tighnabruaich and I know not where else.

On that bright June morning, I remember boarding the boat at Gourock with the keenest anticipation, and although cloud and a few showers met us in the Kyles of Bute, I wasn't disappointed. The lovely, lonely shores of Bute and Cowal, backed by an ever-changing panorama of mountain and forest, passed so close before our eyes that our journey combined the freedom and spaciousness of sea travel with the variety and intimacy of detail one experiences by land.

It was around 12.30pm when we disembarked, along with our kit, at East Tarbert. We took a local bus across the two-mile-long isthmus to the head of Loch Tarbert. There, tucked in at a little pier under the trees, MacBrayne's vessel *RMS Clansman* was waiting to take us on the second stage of our journey. We were particularly glad to see that ship, since we'd booked lunch aboard it, and it wasn't long before we were sitting down to a pleasant and civilised meal while watching the shores of Loch Tarbert glide past the portholes.

The party that sat down together to that meal was the sort of party that almost guarantees a pleasant camp. We were about 18 in number, and pleasantly varied in age and experience, including Michael Daman, Chris Calow, David Francis, John Atkinson, Tony Wilkinson and Andrew Baron to provide the verve and problems for the next 10 days, and a distinguished senior company of David Croxon, Robert Stott, Bernard O'Brien, Peter Holme, Nigel Cleworth and Steven Ashworth to solve those problems and do the work. And so it worked out. For myself, I had on the Isle of Islay about the easiest and idlest of all the camps I've ever attended.

The sea was calm that day, the view wide, and the ship was both trim and comfortable. These MacBrayne vessels that sail the seas around the Hebrides aren't designed for crowds of unruly day trippers, but for local people travelling regularly for shopping and on business. Vandalism and damage are out of the question, so elegant crockery is provided in the restaurant. The washrooms are clean and well fitted, and I remember, on this particular ship, the comfort of the lounge with its deep armchairs and flowery curtains. After we had a paid a brief call at the Isle of Gigha, I sat there in the lounge for a long time, watching the sea and sky, looking for a break in the clouds as we sailed westwards, away from the hills. Sure enough, as so often before and since, it came before us. Over the Isle of Jura and the eastern, hilly half of Islay, the sky was grey, but the western, flatter part of the island was clear, and so as we sailed into Port Ellen, we also sailed into sunshine.

There was the usual busy disembarkation of us, our kit and the island supplies. A minibus took us a mile or so eastwards to where, through the good offices of the local tourist association, I had the promise of a campsite.

It was a good site – not one of our best, perhaps, but good enough. We established ourselves on a shelf of flattish land some 50 yards from the sea. Directly in front of us was a low cliff some 20 feet high. No doubt the sea had washed up against it in the distant past. Now, in front of the cliff lay a patch of rough pasture – too rough for tents – with a rocky shore forming a little, stony inlet. Behind our tents, the land ran up into mile upon mile of rough moorland, studded with small farms where a few acres of pasture housed small herds of various cattle. (In Chris Calow's expert view, they were 'ill-assorted' cattle.)

Port Ellen is one of the busier of those delightful little Hebridean ports we've come to know in the Western Isles, within easy walking distance to be our source of supplies. Our only problem at the site was the water supply. A pipe flowing into an ancient stone trough by the roadside provided a plentiful and convenient supply, but it was far from clean. We rarely minded a little peat in the water that went into our breakfast porridge on camp, but we had to draw the line at tiddlers swimming in the water.

The rocky shore, however, facing south and south-east, provided plenty of driftwood. Some of that wood went for cooking, while the rest provided the source of a succession of cricket bats for our exceedingly crude form of the game, which was played for many hours along the shelf in front of the tents. A perilous game it was for the fielders. From a well-struck stroke, there was no retreat for those fielding on the off-side, save down the cliff, while those on the leg-side had their run impeded by tents and guy lines. There were, of course, many bruises. As to cooking, we aspired to an oven at this camp, since we'd luckily located an asbestos chimney of perfect length, sitting there on the shore at Portnahaven. That piece of kit proved quite successful. Two splendid roasts of pork and beef came out of that contraption, as well as a number of jam tarts.

In addition to being one of the largest of the Inner Hebrides, Islay is also one of its more prosperous, with a population of more than 3,000. We soon discovered that the basis of its prosperity lies principally in the eight whisky distilleries, set in coves and inlets around the coast, with four of them being within a couple of miles of our site. A tour of inspection of the nearest Laphroaig distillery provided an interesting and instructive afternoon for most of us, but despite what we had been led to believe, no free samples were on offer. Such a pity, since the unblended products of Islay Mist and Laphroaig are drinks to offer to connoisseurs, like us! The inspection also provided unexpectedly an introduction and invitation to the Episcopal church on Islay from the man who showed us round the Laphroaig distillery. (See top photograph on page 91.) Harry Newman, a Yorkshireman by birth, was much more interested in the church than in whisky, and with the greatest enthusiasm and goodwill, he arranged for three cars and vans to pick us up on the Sunday and take us to morning service at Bridgend, some 12 miles away. (It was, incidentally, at Islay House in Bridgend that the then Prime Minister, Edward Heath, spent a short holiday a few weeks after his appointment.) After the service, the congregation – mostly expatriate English people – remarked that it seemed just like home to hear the English voices of choirboys.

I've strayed away from the matter of Islay's comparative prosperity. Apart from whisky and cattle, clams also form part of the island's economy. These tasty molluscs are de-shelled in Port Ellen and exported to France, while the shells themselves are simply dumped on the island. Great piles of these attractive shells (so useful as ashtrays) are an occasional but characteristic feature of the Islay scene. We came across our first pile on a walk I took on our only wet afternoon, with Chris, Michael, David and John. That walk sticks clearly in my mind. Nothing particularly dramatic happened, but it seemed full of incident and discovery: the clam shells, an island couple with whom we chatted, a ruined chapel, our disturbing of a large pheasant, discovering a cairn that we thought must mark an ancient burial, and being followed home by a large and affectionate cat. Perhaps it was the company that made the walk interesting to me. I wonder if they still remember it?

Another walk I remember was a sheer delight. One glorious morning, we hired a small coach to take us five or six miles to the southern end of the Big Strand, that marvellous beach that runs unbroken for seven miles along the shore of Loch Indaal. On that gorgeous June morning, there was – as far as the eye could see – only one other person on the beach, and he (or she) was at least a mile away. We swam and picnicked, and then set off to walk along the northern shore of the Oa (curiously pronounced 'Oh'), a peninsula that runs south-west from the edge of the Big Strand. We were making for a point some four or five miles distant, where caves were marked on the map, and all the way, we were winding along the cliff top with the pure blue water of Loch Indaal below us. Across the water, the Rinns of Islay lay peacefully in the sun. We passed delightful sandy coves with slopes of smooth grass behind them. There were rocks to scale and chasms to stride across, and precipices to avoid and wild goats to race. We ran up the heights and came eventually to an area of impressive caves and clefts and arches. The only cave we could actually enter proved to be the lair of the wild goats. We turned quickly away and clambered up to the lip of a chasm, where Bob took some pictures of birds nesting on the ledges. My nerves were suffering as there were too many boys near too many precipices. That was the only drawback to one of the finest walks I ever recall.

On another glorious day, we had a coach trip to Bowmore, the island's first capital, with its famous and much-photographed round church, where we stopped. Some of us later discussed the beer in a pleasant pub, The Westwards, while others gazed at the quiet pastures of the Rinns to Kilchoan Bay, sometimes known as the Machir Bay. The *machir*[iv] was there all right – a soft, grassy carpet of which there was a lovely stretch at the end of the road. The coach pulled up with the lovely green underfoot, and we tumbled out, sleepy with the sun, before picnicking and lying on the vivid, scented carpet of wild thyme, yellow bedstraw and bird's-foot trefoil, its yellow flowers clustering together beautifully. Some of us even dozed for a time, while others swam in the breakers that rolled off the Atlantic and up the glorious beach.

---

iv. *Machir*, or *machair*, is a swathe of soft, grassy land, which is normally found adjacent to coastlines in the Inner and Outer Hebrides. Flat *machir* makes for ideal campsite terrain.

I was the last man off the sand, and as I walked up the beach feeling marvellous, I got into conversation with the only other people in sight. They were a couple who were regarding the splendid scene around us with all too evident disfavour.

"Have you seen owt tropical here?" said the man in a clear Lancashire accent. "We heard on the telly that this were a tropical island."

I told him that I hadn't seen anything strictly tropical on Islay. But feeling cheated by the promise of a tropical island, the couple clearly had no eye nor appreciation for anything else. The incident sticks in my mind as a parable of the perverse side of human nature.

But Islay seemed good enough to us. We dawdled onwards in the coach, down to the village of Portnahaven at the south-west tip of Islay. Of all the sleepy villages one might encounter, this was the sleepiest. It wasn't only sleepy – it also felt a little sad. For this was a village in obvious decay. Many cottages stood empty, while others were already tumbling down. There were no children to be seen, and two old women to whom I chatted at a cottage door told me that only pensioners now live in Portnahaven. Apparently, Portnahaven was founded as a fishing village for the crofters who were cleared off large areas of Islay in the early 19th century. For a generation or two, the men made a living off herring fishing, but at some stage, the herring simply disappeared from the local waters. Ever since, the village has slowly been dying. It was a typical story of the Hebrides.

Our other coach outing was to Port Askaig on the eastern side of Islay, a point at which the ferry runs across to Jura. Once again, we stopped and shopped at Bowmore, but on this day, the weather was less kind. It was raining when we reached Port Askaig, and we took our picnic under the cover of a little bus shed. Afterwards, I called in the trim little pub to see if we could get some coffee, and I remember the surprise of the landlord when I mentioned that we were 19 in number.

"Nineteen!" he said. "Where have you come from? How've you got here?" (He hadn't seen our coach.)

However, we did get our coffee, and when the rain stopped, some of us had a swim in the deep water off the pier. Gordon Smith recovered a sea urchin.

As I've said, our camp was only a mile or so from Port Ellen, and we were often there, watching the ferry come and go. She was a fine sight as she rounded the little islands in the bay. There were half a dozen shops and a couple of pubs in Port Ellen. We made the Islay Hotel our usual rendezvous. The licensing laws of this establishment were all its own and appeared to be roughly that no one under 15 might drink beer, and that persons under 13 might not sit in the public bar, but only in the cocktail bar. One morning, on my first visit to the place, I found our entire company playing darts in the public bar, and it was with both embarrassment and extreme courtesy that the landlord asked me if the very smallest boys might be requested to move into the cocktail bar. Below the cocktail bar was a café called the Waterfall Room. It was a rather attractive place where, on one of the last evenings, we all enjoyed a supper of egg and chips after a football match against the lads of Port Ellen. This was arranged and negotiated by Gordon Smith, who had quickly formed a wide acquaintance among the local youths and maidens. However, having brought the challenge and persuaded us to accept, Gordon withdrew from the proceedings himself, leaving the rest of us to fight the actual battle.

The match was played out on a decent playing field – with goalposts and everything – but the first 10 minutes or so were played under a referee who, having neither whistle nor any semblance of authority, was invariably overruled. A stronger character with a whistle then appeared, and things improved. Since I had the right kind of polo-necked jersey, I was thereby appointed goalkeeper, and therefore had a good and, for most of the time, detached view of the proceedings. These, so far as our team was concerned, consisted in hunting in a kind of pack – led by Bob, Peter and David Croxon – with only Bernard left behind to keep me company and, when necessary, to afford some kind of protection. This was particularly appreciated when the Islay team's right winger – a large, swift and vigorous young man – bore down upon me. Despite Bernard's protection, I let in five goals. However, I can plead in extenuation that I was disconcerted by the bad language that kept breaking out among Islay's supporters (with an average age of about six) who clustered round my goalposts. This was a phenomenon I also observed, some years later, among the infants of Wigtown, who came out with language normally reserved for squaddies from the Gorbals. I should add, however, that we scored four goals, so our defeat was no disgrace. Chris Calow was brought on at half-time as a substitute and was off again – following an injury – after 25 seconds, without even having touched the ball.

For me, as I've said, this was a leisurely, peaceful camp, as I think it was for all of us. There were no accidents I can recall (though I did hear afterwards that Nigel Hardiker got cramp while swimming and was rescued by Peter) and no illness, save an evening's appendix flare-up for David Francis. I never had to raise my voice in rebuke. The voice most heard was that of Chris, though even this was silent for a period of some 15 hours (including sleeping time) in the course of a silence competition with John Atkinson that, against all odds, Chris won.

The weather was kind to us, and so were the local people, though we didn't seem to have quite so much contact with them as at some of our other camps. My most instructive conversation was with the bank manager at Port Ellen, who told me a good deal about the island's economy and its way of life. As an elder of the kirk, he gave us permission to sleep in the church hall on our last evening on Islay, in order to be ready for the morning boat.

And that was how our camp ended, save for the journey home. A rail strike had started, and it was apparent there were going to be no trains to take us home from Glasgow. However, luck remained on our side – as it had done on so many camps before. We managed to locate a local coach company that agreed to provide a driver who would meet us at Gourock and drive us safely back to Rochdale.

But before we all piled on the coach, we still had time for one final, lovely sail. That last afternoon, we glided over the still and sparking waters of Loch Fyne, through the Kyles of Bute and, in glorious sunshine, sailed across the River Clyde to Gourock.

There, as agreed the coach was waiting for us. By now, it was 4.30pm, and we lost no time in packing ourselves in and starting the long drive home. Chris was sure he'd be sick on such a long journey home, but we packed him in the front seat and gave him my treasured 'Islay ship' (a gift from the campers) to look after, and he did very well. Around 10.30pm, we stopped in Keswick for late night fish and chips, and around 1.30am, we drew up safe and sound at home, outside the church hall at Kirkholt.

Listening to the wireless in the coach, we were astonished to hear that all the cricket matches in England had been washed out by rain that day. In Scotland, however, our day had been glorious. And this, we gathered later, had been typical of the last two weeks: sun in Scotland, or at least in the Western Isles, but rain in England – especially in the south! I must record this testimony to the fact that it doesn't always rain in Scotland, not even when it's raining further south.

# Chapter 2

It was a pleasant surprise to me when, in the early summer of 1968, I secured a site in the Isles of Scilly for an August camp. I had thought it almost impossible to find a site nowadays in those fortunate islands, especially at short notice, but when I wrote to Troy Town Farm on the island of St Agnes, we were accepted. The only qualification was that the burning of wood fires was now forbidden on the island, so our first task was to acquire a number of gas stoves and supports to house them, as well as working out new some cooking techniques for our party of 18.

The second major task was to arrange the plan for such a long journey. Since our last visit to the Scillies, the train services to Penzance had been altered. It was no longer possible to arrive in the early morning in time for the sailing of *The Scillonian* at 9.30am. It seemed we'd have to spend a night in Penzance. That took a considerable amount of correspondence from our end, along with kind co-operation from the other, in order to arrange – with the vicar of St John's Church, Penzance – to borrow the church hall there for a night's stay. Since these arrangements were only completed just in time, I had some anxiety before our departure, especially as it seemed that I was going to be alone with a party of 15 boys – all of them young and most without experience. I was relieved when, just a few days before the camp, Frank Hammond and Harold Murphy confirmed that they'd be able to join us.

I remember little of the overnight journey by train, but the events of the few hours after our arrival in Penzance are imprinted on my memory. It was around noon when we arrived on a hot, sunny morning. Our first task was to look out for the local Guide captain who had kindly promised to meet us to show us the hall and arrange lunch in a restaurant. There she was on the platform; she proved most welcoming, kindly and helpful. The trouble was that her mind and mine seemed to work on different wavelengths, and by a different kind of logic, so for the next two hours all was confusion.

Our Guide captain shot off from the station, accompanied by two of our boys, still carrying packs. The rest of us – with the remainder of the kit, either to shoulder or load onto a couple of station trollies – were left behind. When we emerged from the station, there was no sign of our pathfinders. Harold asked the way to St John's Hall, and we were directed, after several enquiries, along a maze of busy, narrow streets, each steeper than the last. It was hot that day, and we had heavy trollies to push along, while dodging both traffic and throngs of holidaymakers. We were drenched with sweat by now, and as once before in Penzance, I started to fear an imminent coronary. Eventually, we reached St John's Hall, but clearly something was wrong: St John's Hall proved to be the Penzance town hall. I could hardly believe that this was what we were borrowing for the night. So, more enquiries ensued. We then discovered that what we really needed was St John's church hall – a quite different place – "down near the station". Off we went, only to realise the hall wasn't near the station at all, but was, in fact, concealed among a maze of old streets. We finally found the hall, only to discover it to be locked, and there was still no trace of our Guide captain or her two companions. Our next move was to find the vicar. This meant first locating the church itself, and then the vicarage. Once found, however, he happily gave us the key to the hall. After that, I barely remember what happened. Somehow, more by luck than judgement, we eventually all got together at the Chinese restaurant where we ordered lunch, hours after the originally agreed time. I was the last to arrive and was greeted with little pleasure by the weary waiters. Lunch wasn't much good either.

After lunch, we shopped and supped and slept comfortably enough in the hall.

On a sunny but windy morning, we were down in good time at the quay where *The Scillonian* was berthed. The first indication of forthcoming trouble was a notice chalked by the gangway: "Weather conditions very rough!"

As we went on board, we heard one of the crew say something about it being the "roughest crossing this year". One of the boys thought this was a joke, and laughed, but the sailor turned to me and said it wasn't funny. "You'll need to keep a close eye on these boys," he said. "It's going to be rough out there."

It was all right for the first half-hour or so, while in the lee of Land's End, but then, as a brisk northerly wind caught us, the waves began to rise, and the fun really started. I took the first two victims of seasickness to the toilet. When I returned to my seat, the rest of our group was suffering. Phillip Davies was prone on the deck. I struggled to get him onto a seat, and that effort set me going too. Soon, I too was slumped in my chair. Phillip and someone else collapsed by my side, and all around were bodies in various stages of distress. The smell was formidable. This was generated by not only our party but virtually everyone on board. Frank Hammond, however, his eyes fixed on the horizon and arms folded tight, remained motionless during the entire sail. He was one of the very few exceptions not to succumb to vomiting, and even he confessed later that it had been a real struggle. Not having suffered seasickness since crossing the Atlantic in 1942, I had forgotten how ill one can feel, as well as how feeble and utterly indifferent to everything one becomes. It was with the greatest relief that I eventually noticed the water growing a little calmer as we drew into the lee of the Scillies.

We had around half an hour on calmer waters, long enough for most of us to enjoy the sight of the islands, as we wove among them. By then, most of our group were feeling better, and after we landed, we enjoyed a lunch in the Sunset Restaurant on the quayside. But some of the boys were still a little queasy and not looking forward to the final stage of our journey from St Mary's, across the sound, to the island of St Agnes – our final destination. It was still more discouraging when we heard that, on account of the heavy seas, the normal launches weren't running to the small islands, so we'd have to travel on the mail launch, *The Tean*, which attempts to get through whatever the weather. We watched with some apprehension as our kit was transferred by crane from *The Scillonian* to *The Tean*.

When we boarded *The Tean* at about 2pm, we noticed – with even more apprehension – that part of the boat seemed to be missing. Between the bottom of the gunwale and the deck was a gap all round of some five or six inches. We soon understood the reason for this apparent deficiency. The water breaking over the boat went out again through this gap, and a huge quantity of water did actually break over it on that trip. Seats and various bits of superstructure provided a refuge for our feet and kit, while water swirled over the deck. But once we had got used to this arrangement and realised *The Tean* was unlikely to sink, I think we all enjoyed that final part of the trip. We bobbed, pitched and rolled in all directions, but at least there was no trace of seasickness now, just a sense of fun and excitement. Eyes that had been blurry and glassy on *The Scillonian* were now as sparkling as the sun and the sea below. We were a merry throng when we landed on the eastern side of St Agnes, near a sand bar that joins the island to its little neighbour, Gugh.

Now, after the trials of the journey, all was well. The sky was blue, the sun was warm, and our transport was waiting to carry the kit to Troy Town Farm. We walked happily, without haste, along that little road that the islanders themselves had constructed. There were expressions of delight at the scene, which opened out around us: flower-filled hedges, trim cottages, and glimpses of the coast and sea in all directions. In 20 minutes, we were at our site: two small fields, side by side, with one for the tents and the other for the games, with only a wall dividing them from the rocky shore. Behind us were tall hedges of escallonia and viburnum, and also the bulb fields of Troy Town Farm. To our right was the small quay at Periglis, with the church beside it, and ahead was a panorama of islands including Annet, the bird sanctuary; Samson; Bryher; Tresco; and in the distance, St Martin's. It was as magnificent a seascape as one could ever wish to see, and there it was in front of us, each and every day.

To our left, there was nothing apart from the coast stretching down to the south-west tip of St Agnes. We were the last people on the island, and therefore – except for the lighthouse keepers on Bishop Rock – we were the last people in Britain. Since Richard and Phillip Davies occupied the most south-westerly of our tents, we accorded them the title of being 'the last people of all in the British Isles'. They seemed pleased with such a distinction.

As soon as we arrived on that sun-baked afternoon, we had a piece of good luck. We discovered in the corner of our field a stout, wooden platform, some five feet square. It was of unknown provenance, but it suited our needs exactly. It would form an ideal base for our rather complicated arrangement of gas stoves and windscreens. It would be ideal since our usual campfires were forbidden on the island, and the stoves would be our means of cooking. When all the stoves were in operation, our galley was quite an impressive sight, catching the admiration of a psychiatrist and his family, who were camping in the next field. No doubt the psychiatrist was a man of experience in his own arena, but he appeared to be a novice camper, overcome by the casual expertise of our youngsters.

He was but one of the interesting people whom we bumped into during the holiday. Another was the Prime Minister, Harold Wilson. Mr Wilson, as usual, was staying on St Mary's for his holidays, and although I didn't see him myself, I heard that one of our shopping parties had literally bumped into him outside the local post office and that Tony Layton had spoken sharply (or more?) to the PM's dog for barking at him.

That was the limit of our contact with Mr Wilson, but we did get on more friendly terms with the Earl and Countess of Onslow. This happened after church on the Sunday. We had observed in the church magazine that one of the two sidesmen of St Agnes was the Earl of Onslow. But my own sense was that neither of the men who had taken the collection that morning looked particularly like an earl. On the other hand, a man in the congregation sporting an old blazer and disreputable trousers, and with a yachting cap under his arm, looked exactly like an earl. And so he turned out to be. After the service, the countess charmed us with her friendly and motherly personality, while the earl hovered in the background, looking as if his feet were killing him and as if he were longing for a drag. Since my impression of earls derives entirely from PG Wodehouse's character Clarence Threepwood, the ninth Earl of Emsworth, this gentleman fitted the bill exactly.

We also met the organist, who was the northern editor of the *Daily Mail*, and after the service, I renewed my acquaintance with Miss Quick, the ornithologist, at her charming cottage across the road. Five years earlier, Bill Farrar, Harold Murphy and I had sat in Miss Quick's garden, talking about flowers and drinking her wonderful elderflower champagne. Now, once again, Miss Quick produced a bottle of homemade wine, as fine as any hock. This time, our conversation was of ghosts and hauntings.

On the whole, the weather at this camp wasn't as good as what we had enjoyed on previous visits to the Scillies. Nevertheless, my impression is one of long, sunny afternoons. One day was spent on the beach, combing along the shore in front of us. We divided into parties, each looking for different kinds of flotsam and jetsam. We found cuttlefish, sea-worn glass, bleached shells and twisted driftwood. We spent hours on this task, and there was a competition for the best collection and arrangement. This, I remember, was won by young Anthony, one of the two guests whom we had taken at the request of the Oldham Probation Service. On another sunny afternoon, we walked to Beady Pool and spent a long time searching for beads of brown Venetian glass spilled there in their thousands from a wrecked ship, centuries ago. And yet another day, we picnicked at the southern tip of Gugh, beside a steep but not too dangerous headland. It was a fine sight watching Frank lead the party up the crag, while Harold took excellent photographs from above and below. We ended that afternoon with an excellent swim at the isthmus that joins St Agnes to Gugh. (As I write, I have a picture of Gugh hanging on the wall in my study.)

Supplies were a bit of a problem on St Agnes. Water, for instance, was in short supply as the pump beside our field often ran dry. So, we used as little fresh water as we could and did all our washing up in sea water. We all remember the disastrous lunch when the water buckets got mixed up, and we had salt water in our coffee and rice pudding – ugh! And the one breakfast time: by the time we had made the porridge, there wasn't a drop of fresh water left, and the well was dry. So, for our breakfast drink, we had to share our only drinkable liquid left – and that was two pints of beer. There was much talk about 'beer for breakfast', but in reality, it didn't go down too well. For other supplies, there was one shop on St Agnes, but it was poorly stocked, so every couple of days we had to send a shopping party to St Mary's. Our means of travel was the one boat stationed on St Agnes, *The Gloria,* whose sailing times were both vague and variable. Each time a party went to St Mary's, I wondered if and when they'd return. But there were no genuine misadventures, and the boys seemed to like the romance of shopping by boat.

The only other *facility* on St Agnes was the Old Coastguard Restaurant, which had seen better days, but where one could still order a large pot of tea to drink at the tables in its sleepy, sun-filled garden. As we left our site for the last time on the morning of our homecoming, I slipped in there, with the rearguard of our party. All the work was now done, and we had plenty of time. The sun blazed, and I enjoyed one of those rare, idyllic half-hours of blissful tranquillity that have a particular place in the memory of all these years of camping.

Despite the excellent help of Frank and Harold, I found the St Agnes camp hard work, chiefly because cooking on gas stoves needs constant supervision. There was a precarious element about it too, so we invented a character called Basil to take the blame for any mishaps. He upset the porridge one morning, and of course, it was Basil who put the salt water in the rice pudding. Of the real members of the party, young though they were and without much experience, there were few who didn't make themselves useful, and it was on St Agnes that I saw the first signs of qualities of competence and good humour in the four or five boys who became the mainstays of our subsequent camps. This party held a promise for the future that was fulfilled. All the same, it was hard work, and I remember that, when we had got back to Penzance and had supped and slept once more in the same hall, I wasn't sure whether I was awake or asleep.

But that is anticipating our return. There are a few more incidents to recall from the St Agnes camp. Ghost stories in the store tent one night caused so much alarm to one of our Oldham boys that he knocked me up at midnight in search of reassurance. The lighthouses caused some consternation too, flickering light over the camp at night-time. And on a damp, misty day on Tresco, we walked around the island and watched the breakers crashing on the rocky northern shore, but we couldn't find the entrance to Piper's Hole – a site we had been seeking. Then, there was the morning when the news broke of the Soviet invasion of Czechoslovakia, which we heard on Harold's little radio.

Being somewhat tied to the stove, I missed most of the morning expeditions – which were usually devised and led by Frank, Harold and Graham Hill – so I suspect I missed a great deal of fun. But it was pleasurable enough to be pottering in the camp field, enjoying marvellous views, breathing the lovely flower-scented air or watching oystercatchers tread along the shore. Our psychiatrist friend said it was the most beautiful campsite he could ever have imagined. I thought of St David's, Tobermory and Catacol on the Isle of Arran, and I found it hard to decide if he was right.

It was a long journey home, of course. We left Troy Town Farm early one morning and walked across St Agnes before taking *The Gloria* to St Mary's. There, we had time to shop and make our lunch of soup and coffee on gas stoves by the quay. We watched our kit safely slung aboard *The Scillonian*, and then, with some apprehension, we remembered our outward journey as we boarded. This time, our fears were groundless. The sailing was calm and placid, and we reached Penzance around 8pm in the evening. There was another spell of graft as we shunted our kit to the church hall once more, before making supper and preparing rations for the following day. I recall how good it felt to lie down at last, to sleep even on the bare floor of the church hall.

We woke in good time, had breakfast and then cleaned up, before shifting the kit to the station once more. The 9am train from Penzance left perfectly on time, and save for the occasional interruption to dole out sandwiches, we sat back, either dozing or listening to the Test match on Harold's radio. Others idly watched stretches of the English countryside pass by under a warm August sun. At last, by evening, we arrived back in Manchester to the happy welcome of parents and friends, bringing us all back to life once more.

# Chapter 3

I can't for the life of me remember why we picked the Isle of Coll. It may have been the fact that, in 1968, Tiree and Coll – adjacent islands in the Inner Hebrides – had the highest total hours of sunshine in the whole of Britain. Or it may have been my reading of James Boswell's account of his visit to Coll with Dr Samuel Johnson in Boswell's Journal of a *Tour to the Hebrides with Samuel Johnson, LL.D 1773.*[8] Or then, I may have simply read an intriguing description in a guidebook. Whatever it was, something commended Coll and persuaded 19 of us to join the party, including a number of first-timers, namely John Butterworth, Ian Aitchison, Stephen Andrews, Glenn Bratby and Paul Stone. On the side of experience, however, we had Nigel Cleworth and Frank Hammond, and I think Michael Daman and David Francis came next in camp experience.

It took a good deal of correspondence with the Scottish Tourist Board and with shipowners, Messrs David MacBrayne, to find a site on Coll and arrange the details of the journey. Eventually, a letter arrived from the proprietor of the Coll Hotel, Mr Alistair Oliphant, promising us a site near Arinagour, the island's main village. Meanwhile, Messrs MacBrayne combined with British Rail to provide an interesting and enjoyable itinerary. Once again, it was a matter of meeting at our church hall, late on a Monday night, with a number of obliging fathers agreeing to drive us to Manchester. By 8am on the Tuesday morning, we had arrived at Glasgow Central Station.

Then came a bit of panic, since we realised our train for Oban left not from Glasgow Central, as we had been informed, but from Glasgow Queen Street, a good 10-minute walk away. We didn't have much time to spare. We bundled Nigel into a taxi, and before the driver had time to protest, piled the heaviest kit on top of him in the rear. The rest of us, still well-loaded, scampered as best we could through the city's busy morning streets for what seemed like an age. But we made it, and as soon as we got to Glasgow Queen Street, even before the train had left the station, we seemed to get an early impression of the Highlands and the west. I don't know what it is; perhaps it's the kind of people who are travelling there, or maybe the names on the indicator boards, but there's a world of difference between Glasgow Central and Glasgow Queen Street stations. Glasgow Central smacks of the city and business, while Queen Street hints of imminent lochs, glens and the western sea.

And so we moved off in good heart up the famous West Highland Line, along the north shore of the Clyde, where there's so much to see, including those geese acting as watchdogs at one of the whisky warehouses. We then passed up the wooded side of Loch Long, where one first feels the scale and grandeur of the Highlands. Then, it's across by Arrochar and Tarbert to the northern reaches of Loch Lomond. It was around here when I suggested to Frank and Nigel that a swift mid-morning glass of beer would be welcome. They agreed, and we moved into the refreshment car, and in minutes, of course, we were joined by the rest of the party.

There was no one else in the car at first, then a man came in, and by an odd coincidence, we knew him – at least, I did. He was the Chief Scout. I couldn't help breathing a sigh of relief that we were, for the first time, not a Scout party, but a Sigma party. Not that I have anything against the Chief Scout, and had we been Scouts, I expect he'd have been very nice to us. Nevertheless, I was reflecting anxiously on the forms and documents we hadn't obtained, and on rules we might unwittingly be breaking. But now, as Sigma, we owed allegiance to no man nor organisation, and it was with insouciance that I watched Chris Callow request the gentleman's autograph. Having no wish, however, to discuss the rival merits of the Scouts and Sigma with the Chief Scout, or anyone else, I firmly suppressed Chris's suggestion that he should introduce the Chief Scout to the chief of Sigma.

Instead, we got talking to a Scotsman on board about the Campbells and Ben Cruachan, about the Pass of Brander, and about the history and romance of this awesome and beautiful land we were passing through.

With this lively conversation, and with so much to see on that sunny morning, the journey passed quickly. Around noon, we dropped down into Oban, and soon afterwards, we were lunching, thankfully, in the station restaurant.

After lunch, we found a more attractive café on the seafront and booked a tea of fish and chips for later. Then, it was a matter of buying the things I always forget (such as torch batteries), followed by a good, long stretch of leisure. While most of the party were exploring Oban – climbing the hillside to McCaig's Folly or boating in the harbour, where a submarine lay anchor – Nigel, Frank and I spent a relaxing time, lying on the pier in the sunshine. I couldn't help remembering that, only 24 hours earlier, I had been shopping in Manchester in miserable murk and rain. Now, there was nothing around but peace, beauty, leisure and sun. And in such a frame of mind, hard though the boards of the pier were, I fell asleep. I was awakened eventually by the familiar voice of one of our church members, Harold Wilkinson, who was holidaying in Scotland and was less surprised to see us than I was to see him, since he had already met some of our party in the town.

A splendid tea followed. Then, after a final stroll round Oban, we found our ship, the *RMS Claymore*, on which we were to sail to the Isle of Coll at 7am the following morning. We had booked inexpensive cabins on board for the night, and once we had surmounted a few difficulties caused by the onset of rain and a harassed stewardess – and Chris had finally tried on his life jacket – we settled in for good night's sleep.

I woke just before 7am to a lovely morning, with the sun shining through my porthole, and was soon on deck in time to watch us sail away. We then enjoyed an ample, leisurely breakfast in the ship's civilised and rather old-fashioned restaurant. The rest of the party all looked well rested and smart. It struck me how appropriate our dark-blue Sigma jerseys looked in that setting – ideal for group ship travel.

We had the pleasure of watching the shores of the Isle of Mull and Morvern drift by. As we came nearer to Tobermory, Frank and I spotted landmarks remembered from our camp there in 1962, including Salen and Duart Castle, along with Calve Island and its nearby heronry, then Aros Headland (where we'd camped), before, finally, the beautiful Tobermory Bay and Tobermory (see bottom photograph on page 91) itself. Nothing there seemed to have changed – not even the weather, for a sudden shower reminded us of what Mull had been like in 1962. Soon, we pulled away from Tobermory again, and the waters widened out beyond Ardnamurchan Point, the most westerly point on the British mainland. Now, we were really sailing the Hebrides, and it was pure joy.

Not long after 10am, Coll came into view, and half an hour later, we were unloading our kit onto the pier at Arinagour and meeting the pier master in full kilt, as well as the hotel landlord (Mr Oliphant) and the shopkeeper (Mr Sproat). We knew the population of Coll was only around 120, but even so, I hadn't realised how big an event the arrival of our party of 19 would be. Everyone was so welcoming to us, as if we were old friends returning, rather than strangers arriving.

Our site was on a piece of open moorland, rather than pasture, some 100 yards above and behind the Coll Hotel (see top photograph on page 92). We looked down on Arinagour: first, at the kirk close to us; then, at the whitewashed hotel; and along the shore to a row of tiny cottages with rusty, corrugated-iron roofs. Beyond Arinagour lay miles and miles of sea, with glimpses in the distance of the Treshnish Islands and parts of the coast of the Isle of Mull. It was another splendid, beautiful site, very close to the village and sheltered, we thought, from the prevailing westerly winds by the hill behind us. It wasn't long before we had the tents up and were well established. By mid-afternoon, I had a party on the sands on the far shore of Coll seeking, and finding, supplies of driftwood.

It had been a grand day, but by nightfall, cirrus cloud had already started to build above. And despite the reassurances of two locals that the weather was set fair, I wasn't at all surprised to be wakened in the morning by sounds of rain and a considerable wind. I got up at 7.30am, and 15 minutes later, that wind had become a roaring gale. Pegs and brailing pegs were popping out all over the place, sidewalls were flapping, and rain poured onto the recumbent figures – especially on poor Stephen Andrews, who had the corner position in the most exposed tent. I called on everyone to get up swiftly, but the gale was picking up even more by now. Tent poles started to bend and snap. All we could do at that point was to drop the tents with the occupants still underneath, and leave everyone lying prone under the howling wind, while we rescued our kit and secured the store tent – our biggest and strongest on the entire camp.

The next step was to move everyone into the store tent. Climbing from under the sorry piles of rope and canvas that had once been their tents, the boys came racing for shelter through the piercing rain, wet and bedraggled, with many still in pyjamas and others half-dressed. Although this was his first morning on camp, John Butterworth looked well-dressed and unconcerned, as if he were still at home. So did Ian Aitchison, who was simply amused by the Force 9 wind that had flattened our tents. We all managed to get inside the store tent, and we dried off some of our wettest members before breakfasting on biscuits. Frank presided over a game of '20 questions', which passed the time, but the large tent itself was still flapping alarmingly, and most of us had to sit round the edge, hanging on to the walls and the sodden groundsheets. It was cold work that morning, and we were all soaking. We'd had nothing warm to eat or drink, and by 10.30am, I reckoned if we stayed there much longer someone might get pneumonia.

But where to go for refuge? We were completely new to Coll and knew of no possible refuge except a bothy that had been shown to Nigel by a friendly man called Archie. Nigel didn't exactly speak highly of its amenities – of which there were basically zero – but it seemed better than where we were. So, we made a plan. We sorted out what we'd need to cook a meal, and then everyone grabbed something while Frank and I held the tent door narrowly open against the powerful wind. Seventeen bedraggled figures slipped through the tent door, one by one, and raced down to the village, behind Nigel.

With some difficulty, Frank and I flattened and secured the store tent, and then followed the others to the bothy, with just a moment en route in the Coll Hotel to swallow a much-needed dram. We never got to the bothy, for as we passed the manse at the end of the village street, there inside was Nigel's party, beckoning us to join them. They had been noticed by the minister's wife as they ran past, and she offered us the use of a large room, where the kindly soul was already lighting a fire for us. She couldn't do enough: our soaking clothes had to be hung up, we had to use her kitchen to make coffee and soup, and we must stay as long as we needed. Her kindness only added to our sense of luxury, as we felt the warmth of her fire and prepared our simple meal.

The Church of Scotland minister himself wasn't around, and soon, we learned why. With all the other men of the village, he was out watching the coast, looking for a 14-foot boat being tossed around, somewhere in that boiling sea between Coll and Mull. Early that morning, Coll's other priest – the minister of the Free Kirk – had set out from Mull, and the mailboat had spotted him halfway to Coll, just minutes before the storm struck. His return was, by now, long overdue. Five fishing boats and a lifeboat had joined in the search, as well as, by now, a Royal Air Force Shackleton aircraft, which we spotted several times, circling overhead. Visibility was poor, and we all knew what the sea must have been like. Around noon, as one or two of the men reappeared in the village, with no news of a sighting, the atmosphere began to turn from anxiety to sadness.

"We dinnae give him any hope," one of the villagers said, nodding gravely. He added that, although Mr McIver had been a very good seaman, "In a wee boat like that, he has nae chance."

I think it was around 2pm, however, that we noticed a hint of brightness in the west. Within half an hour, the rain had stopped, and the gale had dropped – thankfully – to a brisk breeze. The sun started shining again. The clearance, however, seemed far too late to be of any help to Mr McIver. We could do nothing but wait, quietly and tensely, for any news to come.

In the meantime, we had to try to retrieve our camp, and this was done remarkably quickly. The brisk wind was soon drying both grass and canvas. Someone found some lengths of scrap iron and timber to replace our ruined tent poles, and we got busy with needle and thread on the scores of rips and holes in the tent walls.

While we were busy rescuing our tents, the remarkable news came through that Mr McIver, somehow, was safe. I don't know how the first rumour arrived, but it was confirmed by one of the Arinagour villagers. It was a godsend, and Mr McIver was safe. His boat had been sighted by the Shackleton, beached and amazingly undamaged, on the northern tip of Coll. Years ago, the village of Sorisdale stood at the most northerly point of the island. But now, like so many dwelling places on Coll, the village is empty and in ruins, save for one cottage where two elderly brothers still live. Of course, there would be no transport for Mr McIver from Sorisdale, so we weren't surprised to see the doctor's van heading off along the lonely road to pick him up. Half an hour later, as the van came back into sight, we all ran down to the road to greet the Free Kirk minister and congratulate him on his remarkable escape.

He turned out to be an elderly man with a fine, rugged face, quite unshaken by his ordeal. "Och," he said, "I'm all right, but how are ye laddies doing? That wind must have made a terrible mess of your tents. If ye're wanting shelter for the night, there's plenty of room in my manse."

We assured him that we too were all right. But it wasn't until the next day when we heard from Mr McIver exactly what had happened. Soon after the storm broke, a wave had swamped his boat and stopped the engine immediately. For four long hours, he had tossed and drifted at sea. With spray flying in his face, he could only see a few yards ahead. But with what must have been superb seamanship, Mr McIver managed to keep his boat afloat. When the wind eased and the spray lifted, he noticed that he was dangerously close to the cliffs of Rhum. It was essential to get his engine going. He succeeded in doing so by drying the starter plug with a piece of cloth torn from his shirt. And so, miraculously, he returned to Coll safely.

That wasn't the end of my memories of Mr McIver. For on the Sunday evening, we attended a service at his church, following a morning service at the nearby Church of Scotland. I had always understood the Free Kirk of Scotland to be a somewhat narrow-minded organisation in which Sabbath-breaking was considered a great sin. One heard more about their stories of hell than those of heaven. The reality, as we found on Coll, was very different. We were welcomed at the door, first by Archie, who had already treated us to gifts of lettuce and fish, and then by Mr McIver himself. We were shown to seats right in front of the pulpit. We soon got used to the special ways of the Free Kirk, where one sits to sing and stands to pray. No musical instrument is thought proper, and the singing is led by a sort of choirmaster who sits directly under the minister's high platform. We then came to the sermon, a long Scots version on the 23rd Psalm, 'The Lord is my Shepherd'. Towards the end of the sermon came a passage I shall never forget.

"Now my friends," said Mr McIver. "Ye ken that, on Thursday, I had a great deliverance from the Lord. And on Friday, the *Daily Express* telephoned and asked me, 'Now, Mr McIver, what were ye thinking during those hours that ye were tossing in the storm?'

"And, me friends, I thought they were a wee bit prying, so I said, 'Och, there's a time for thought and a time for action, and that was a time for action.'

"And then they said, 'But, Mr McIver, ye were in great danger...were ye no afraid?'

"And I said, 'Och, I ken that I was in great danger, but I was no afraid, for I knew that the Lord is my Shepherd.'" And then, leaning forwards and gazing down on our pews with his searching eyes, Mr McIver said, "And ye wee laddies, ye must ne'er be afraid for whatever should happen to ye; ye must know that the Lord is your Shepherd."

The printed word can't do justice to Mr McIver's earnestness and sincerity, nor to the impact of such a message coming from one whose deliverance from the gate of death was so fresh in our minds. I knew, as soon as I heard them, that I'd never forget those words.

After that service – on a lovely, peaceful, sunny evening – Michael and I walked down to the village to beg the loan of some sugar to see us through until morning. At the second cottage, a lady stood at the door, and I put in my request.

"Och," she said, "of course we can lend you some sugar. I dinnae have it myself, but Mrs Kennedy will lend you some," and she called out for Mrs Kennedy.

A motherly, big woman came to the door and immediately found us a bag of sugar. I said we'd return it in the morning, as soon as the shops opened.

"Och," said Mrs Kennedy, "ye'll do nae such thing. Keep it…ye're more than welcome, but wait a wee minute." She then disappeared into the house again and emerged a few moments later with two of the biggest and finest homemade cakes I've ever seen. "Take these," she said. "They'll make a wee piece for the laddies' supper."

There will be more to say about the kindness of the people of Coll, but now a word or two about our adventures. There were bikes for hire at the hotel, and most of our party took advantage of these at one time or another to explore the island. Stephen Francis and John Butterworth went off one afternoon to the northern end, some seven miles off. But on the way back, about a mile from Sorisdale, Stephen's brakes failed on a hill. He went head over heels and right over a small crash barrier by the roadside. His bike was damaged, and Stephen was not only cut and bruised but briefly knocked out too. John ran for help, but he could find no one apart from a deaf old man in a farmhouse, about a mile away. The man came to the scene, straightened the front wheel of the bike and then walked off, with hardly a glance at Stephen. John decided the pair had better walk back to camp, and they walked five miles without seeing a soul. It was David, Stephen's brother, who found them, having set out to see why they were so late for tea. Once located, we soon had them back to camp in the car of the friendly doctor who was holidaying in a nearby cottage. Stephen spent that evening in bed to get over the shock and weariness. We all thought very highly of John, who had stuck with, and helped, his injured fellow cyclist.

A different kind of adventure was our voyage to Staffa (see bottom photograph on page 92). We arranged the private hire of a good-sized boat from Tobermory, which does trips to Staffa and Iona during the holiday season, and we set off one cloudy morning when there was a fair swell. It wasn't long before poor Chris was sitting on an oil drum in the stern, waiting to be sick, but most of us found that, by standing in the open air and keeping our eyes on the horizon, we could master the queasiness. I think Chris was the only victim that day. Meanwhile, Ian Taylor, the boatman, told us it was difficult to land on Staffa and that, so far that year, he had only put one party ashore. However, he hoped we'd all manage it that day, with us being nimble enough to climb down into a dinghy and get ashore that way. In fact, a patch of calm water off the south of Staffa enabled Taylor to bring his own boat right alongside the little concrete quay. We were soon ashore, clambering over those extraordinary hexagonal basalt columns and making our way into Fingal's Cave (see photograph on page 93), made famous in *The Hebrides* overture by Felix Mendelssohn, composed in 1830. In that lonely, impressive place, we sang 'Crimond', with our trebles' voices soaring above the crash of waves and lingering high in the lofty dome of the cave. We made our picnic among the columns by the quay, with a crowd of cormorants looking down from ledges on the cliffside, high above. It had been our intention to explore Staffa later, but rain started to fall, and with a change in wind direction, Ian was anxious to move clear of our rather precarious anchorage. So, we were soon off again and threading our way through the Treshnish Islands, where we spotted the remains of human habitations from long ago, and we sailed past a wall that looked like it had been, at one time, a kind of fortification. We enjoyed not only calmer waters now but also wonderful views of hundreds and hundreds of sea birds. The puffins caught our particular attention (see top photograph on page 94). We also saw seals, and just off coast of Arinagour on Coll, we spotted a couple of huge but harmless basking sharks. As we neared the island, the skipper handed the helm to Stephen, who found steering a steady course at sea not quite as easy as it looks.

The following day, the pier master on Coll said to me, "Terrible queer course that fellow Taylor was steering as ye came back yesterday. I thought it was maybe one of your boys at the helm?" he asked quizzically.

We had to admit it, but whatever the course, it had been an unforgettable sail.

Another day out was provided by the friendly doctor mentioned earlier. He had a large shooting-brake car and offered to take us in two parties to spend a day at one of the beaches on the north-west shore. We gladly accepted, especially since it was a lovely day, blessed by brilliant sunshine. The doctor dropped us by a burn that flows through the *machir* and then on through the sand dunes to a huge, silver bay. I recall the first thing we did was to stroll a little further up the road, to view the scene of Stephen's accident. I was glad we did so, for we got a majestic view of Eigg, Rhum and Canna to the north. We then began to collect wild flowers, which grow so brightly and profusely in the *machir* of Coll. Where the ground had previously been cultivated to make small fields of oats and vegetables, there was a thick carpet of scarlet pimpernel, forget-me-not and bugloss – a brilliant sight. In a little over an hour, we had 65 species in our collection.

A most leisurely and delightful picnic followed, and then several hours of messing about in the burn, stalking in the sand dunes, swimming in the blue sea and constructing elaborate canal systems on the beach. It was a magnificent day, during which we saw just two or three other people.

Unfortunately, the weather that day wasn't typical of our time on Coll. There was no repeat of the gale from the first day, but we had plenty of rain and wind, and one whole day of damp and heavy mist. On that morning, we walked south, this time finding 58 varieties of flowers in an hour and a half. We ended up at a roadside loch, and on the principle that they couldn't get much wetter than they already were,

John Atkinson, Steven Bratby and Paul Stone jumped in, hilariously, fully clad.

It turned gloomy that evening, and Mrs Steward, the wife of the local laird, came to see if we'd like to take shelter in her barn. We weren't in any particular difficulty by then, but it seemed both wise and courteous to have a look. So, Nigel and Frank took a party to inspect the barn, and subsequently, they spent a pleasant evening in the laird's house, watching television, since it was the day of the Prince of Wales's investiture. They were all clearly impressed by an invitation to a Buckingham Palace garden party, which stood proudly on the mantelpiece.

On another cold and bleak evening, we had one of our mad, inventive sessions, which at least kept us warm. We invented the 'Peat Cutters' Song and Dance'. Just above our tents was a peat bed, which was useful for supplementing the driftwood collected on the shore. One of the team, dreamed up an 'old Coll custom', namely that, on the night following Midsummer's Eve, anyone whose surname begins with B must sing a Gaelic song while carrying a short ladder, as well as a rabbit carved in wood. Following this charade, he is then rewarded by gifts from the villagers. Everything about Coll is so improbable that this seemed no less likely than anything else, and so we weren't surprised to find John Butterworth busily carving his rabbit in anticipation of winning the prize. Young Bratby, however, was a little more sceptical, but even his incredulity was shaken the following day when he noticed that, in Arinagour, there was a surprising number of particularly short ladders. (When one thinks of it, ladders are entirely necessary on an island where gales can so frequently lift a roof, and since the dwellings are all cottages, a short ladder is more than useful than a long one.)

On another topic, the boat from Oban calls at Coll on Mondays, Wednesdays and Fridays. Normally, it reaches the pier at about 10.30am, and 20 minutes later, its passengers, mail and supplies arrive in Arinagour. It's only then that the village seems quite busy. That's to say, there may be as many as 20 people and eight vehicles on the village road, along with a further 10 people in the shop and post office.

One day, I went into MacDonald's shop at 12.10pm. It was a Friday. The rush was over by now, and there was no one in but Mr McDonald, who was sitting with his head in his hands, drinking a cup of tea.

"You're tired, Mr MacDonald," I said. "Have you been busy?"

"Och, Canon," he replied – I was called 'Canon' more frequently in a week on Coll, than in a year at home. "'Tis always a terrible rush on the days the boat comes in!"

We tended to split our custom between the two shops on Coll. The second – a small, corrugated-iron building, painted green and red – was owned by the kindly Mr and Mrs Sproat. One day, I was in there when some members of our party were looking for presents to take home. There was, in fact, little choice for presents, but someone spotted a set of small screwdrivers and asked the price.

"How much is this, Annie?" said Mr Sproat to his wife.

She looked at it. "Half a croon," she said. "Say it's half a croon, Willie."

Our prospective young buyer was delighted with the price and promptly bought it. I next saw him outside, examining his purchase. On the back, the price was clearly marked "5/11" (5 shillings and 11 pence – more than twice as much as it had been sold for to one of our campers).

This sort of kindness was typical of Coll, but in addition to such kindness, there was a wonderful sense of trust and courtesy. No one said to me, "See that the boys close the gates," or "Don't let them touch the boats." Everyone trusted us from the moment we stepped ashore on Coll. This trust reached its climax on the final night, which was spent in the new waiting room and store at the end of the pier. Mr Oliphant suggested we should do this in order to catch the boat at the early time of 7am.

When I mentioned it to the pier master, his answer was immediate: "Of course, ye can all sleep there."

And although there were all sorts of goods and packages in the store, no one even asked us to be careful with them. But we did carefully spread our sleeping bags on and among outboard engines, drums of oil and sacks of cement. In the morning, when the pier master arrived – nice and early – to prepare for the ship's arrival, he even apologised for disturbing us.

Perhaps one of the reasons for the islanders' kindness was that youngsters are a rarity on Coll; its population now being down to around 120. We saw no more than half a dozen boys and three girls during our time there. The boys couldn't even raise a football team to play us, but they came up one evening with, I think, five players – all of whom seemed to be called Ian – and joined in our games. Cricket was evidently a novelty to the island children, and our doctor friend heard one the local lads saying, "The boys at the camp are playing some game where ye throw a ball at three sticks."

There are still a few more incidents and people from Coll tucked away in the rag bag of my memory. Neilly John, for instance, was always standing at the door of the first cottage in Arinagour. Apparently, he was responsible for the odd jobs in the village. To judge from a gate he'd constructed, they seemed very odd jobs indeed.

Then, there was the evening when some of our party, out in a boat with Frank, somehow got involved with a coastguard practice, which included the firing of rockets. I wasn't present myself, but it seems Frank's boat party thought they were coming under attack, and being used as 'targets'. I heard some hilarious accounts of such antics.

And on a more serious note, I recall the solemnity and sense of occasion with which the minister at the Church of Scotland asked if the scripture readings at morning service might be done, "by yourself and one of your leading boys". I asked Michael to share with me what must be a rare honour for an English visitor.

I mentioned how we spent our last night in the waiting room at the end of the pier. The floor wasn't exactly comfortable, and I was required to tell stories, for ages, to help get the party to sleep. All the same, we were ready for the boat at 7am, and were somewhat disconcerted to find it didn't arrive. At about 7.30am, the pier master received a message to say it had been held up in Barra and wouldn't now be arriving until around 10am. Since we had planned to breakfast on the boat, this was a minor blow, but we made the best of things. The minister appeared from nowhere and brought milk for a brew. So, for the next hour or so, we entertained the minister, the pier master, one labourer and ourselves with as much as we could remember of our most recent gang show. Tony threw in the poem *The Lion and Albert,*[9] about which, I recall, the minister was very enthusiastic.

The boat came as promised about 10am, filled with a party from Edinburgh University's Training Corps, who had been camping on Barra. Someone christened these, perhaps unfairly, 'the toy soldiers'. The trouble was that this lot had booked the whole of the ship's restaurant for lunch, and since we had already missed breakfast, we weren't too pleased. With some difficulty, I persuaded the purser to lay on a decent snack of coffee and biscuits for us at 11am, and we tucked into this with relish. We were just finishing the snack when the purser came to me again to say that the toy soldiers had cancelled their lunch (probably due to a bit of a swell), and he'd be delighted to accommodate us in their place. So, having got up from a mid-morning snack at 11.30am, we sat down again to lunch some 15 minutes later. The boys did justice to that lunch, with even Chris being persuaded that he wasn't going to be sick again. And he wasn't.

We sailed pleasantly down the Sound of Mull to the sounds of piping by the soldier boys. Unfortunately, at Oban, we found our boat had arrived far too late for us to catch the intended train, and when we eventually left by mid-afternoon, we knew that we wouldn't catch the evening train home from Glasgow. It was 6pm by the time we reached Glasgow, and by now, there was nothing for it but to kick our heels until midnight, with the hope we could leave for Manchester at that time. We didn't much enjoy the next six hours. Glasgow isn't a terribly pleasant place on a Saturday night, especially when one is fresh from the freedom and peace of the Hebrides. Added to the weariness of killing time was the anxiety of wondering if there would be enough room for us on the late train south, especially since we found ourselves on the first Saturday of a Glasgow wakes' week. I had all kinds of negotiations with station officials, including the station master. In the end, an inspector showed us to some seats. He received my grateful thanks, as well as an overly generous tip, before disappearing smartly. It transpired that he had shown us to seats that had already been reserved, and we were promptly slung out again. I didn't think very kindly of Glasgow at that point, especially when a policeman started being officious with members of our team. But it all came right in the end. A kindly guard found us plenty of room, once the train had started moving. We all got comfortable, and my last memory of the journey is of Chris laughing in his sleep. We were soon drawing slowly into Manchester Victoria, early on a Sunday morning, to be welcomed by a bunch of parents with a fleet of waiting cars.

Yet another Hebridean island had been added to our collection. The peaceful land, the silver beaches and the kind people of the Isle of Coll now have their fond place in our memories, along with Arran, Islay and Mull, as well as those from other islands, including Anglesey, St Agnes and Guernsey. For my part, I think it was on Coll that I first felt deeply the lure and fascination of the Hebrides. It's a lure from which I've never recovered.

# Chapter 4

In August 1969, Chris Samuels, my curate at St Thomas', led a small Sigma camp to Downham near Clitheroe in Lancashire. Although certainly part of the Sigma records, the Downham camp doesn't feature in this journal as it isn't among my personal memories. But it does have a connection with what follows, for having camped only once in the summer of 1969 – on the Hebridean island of Coll – I began to find that, by autumn, I was hankering for a few more days in the country before the year ended.

For this reason, a plan – long in the back of my mind – came into the foreground. We'd try a December camp during the heart of winter, directly after Christmas. I'd planned on locating the winter camp at Rhoscolyn on Anglesey for several reasons: first, Rhoscolyn was an obvious choice for us since the journey would be relatively short; second, if anything went wrong, we'd be among friends we knew from previous camps there; third, we'd be virtually surrounded by the western sea and should expect mild winter weather; and finally, the present generation of campers had never been to such a beloved place.

I was surprised to find a number of enthusiasts for the idea. Also, several parents, if not exactly enthusiastic, were at least tolerant of it. Peter Holme promised to come along, and among the younger end were Michael Daman, Tony Layton, David and Stephen Francis, Chris Calow, Kevin Shore, John Atkinson and Andy Holt. (There was plenty of character and experience among that bunch of youngsters.) As Christmas approached, David Croxon and Harry Newman added their names to the list. I knew then there would be nothing to worry about in terms of personnel. Also, by beginning our preparations in good time, we were able to work out exactly what we might need; for example, storm lamps, weatherproof clothing, and stout iron pegs for driving into potentially hard, frosted ground. We'd also have enough time to hire items that we didn't already have ourselves from Messrs Langdon's of Liverpool.

All the same, and despite such early preparations, the last few days before camp were hectic. Christmas Day came on the Thursday, the old people's party on the Saturday, and on Monday, 29th December, we were planning on arriving at Rhoscolyn. Somehow, everything got done on time, and our coach departed for Anglesey at 9.30am on a bitterly cold, grey morning. Charles Daman, Frank Hammond and John Butterworth came along with us, just for the pleasure of the ride.

For the first four hours, there was little pleasure in the journey. The coach was bitterly cold – unsurprisingly, since it had a window missing. The weather was bleak, matched by a dark cloud of anxiety that was brooding over me, if not the others. It's one thing to envisage a winter camp from the safe haven of summer or even autumn, but it's another to set out on one, in the middle of a flu epidemic, in a freezing cold coach on a dark morning with a threat of snow in the air.

Our earlier theories on how we'd get the tents up and how we'd keep warm and dry started to look a little dodgy. And my confidence that we would escape the flu, while camping, began to wane. Matters were made no easier by our reception at Messrs Langdon's when we arrived to pick up our hired kit. It wasn't ready, and we were told, "We didn't actually expect you'd be risking it in this weather."

While the various items were being assembled, one of Langdon's men laughed and asked, "And whose idea was it to take these young lads camping at this time of year?"

I said, "Mine!" with a show of cheerfulness, which wasn't even convincing to me.

However, on we went from Liverpool along the north coast of Wales. It got no warmer, and scuds of snow began. A thick, white frost lay on the fields, and when we stopped for a drink at a roadside café, I tested the ground: it was rock hard. There was just one small ground for hope. The wind was in the south-east, and so if any part of the country was going to escape the worst of cloud and snow, it would be the north-western corner of Wales. Sure enough, as we travelled westwards, it began to happen, as so often before. A brighter prospect began to open up. Around Conway, we noticed the sky had lightened, just a little. And soon after, the first patch of blue appeared. When we stopped in Bangor to buy supplies, there was a distant brightness to the north-west, where Anglesey lay waiting for us.

As we crossed the Menai Bridge, we entered a different world. The frost lay lighter on the fields. The clouds kept thinning. We spotted a few gorse bushes in flower, and the blessed prospect of a sunny evening was coming ever nearer. Even an officious policeman who flagged us down for speeding seemed trifling. We knew the sun would be shining on Rhoscolyn.

And so it was. Well-known landmarks came into view – Valley Crossroads and Four Mile Bridge – and then, finally, at Rhoscolyn Church, my heart leaped. As ever, the church stood there in the afternoon sunshine. Surrounding the church was that panorama of cliffs, quiet lanes and homely fields that had given us such delight over many earlier years. And there to greet us at the gate at Bryn Goleu was Mr Evans. He was the same as ever: bubbling over with his animated talk and energy.

He knew exactly we needed: a site sheltered from that strong south-easterly wind. He had the ideal spot ready for us in the pump field, near the shop. A fine hedge gave the shelter we needed, and as soon as we'd lugged our kit into the lee of the hedge, we immediately felt the difference. After saying *au revoir* to the coach's driver and its three returning passengers, we took barely a few minutes to get the tents up. Soon after, we'd started to get a meal under way.

We had hired two large ridge tents and a dining shelter from Langdon's. In each of the ridge tents, we put four juniors, all except Michael, on a camp bed. Peter, Harry and David each had one of our own larger tents, and I was cosy enough in my Wanderlust. Meanwhile, we placed two layers of groundsheets, with sheets of newspaper between them, on all the tent floors. The camp beds were then covered, with newspaper first and then with a blanket. Next came the sleeping bag, and on top, one, two or even three blankets, depending on need. It was that insulation from the frozen ground that kept us all comfortable. And although it was hard work getting to bed with such a set-up, the result was worth it. We all enjoyed as warm a night's sleep as we'd ever known at any previous camps.

But to go back to the day of our arrival, within an hour or so of our arrival, we were eating a delicious hot meal, outdoors, while watching the sunset behind Rhoscolyn Church. I couldn't get over this contrast to what we'd been expecting a couple of hours before. I remember lingering over my meal until darkness fell.

It was dark before 5.30pm on those winter evenings, but we were never reduced to crouching around the fire or huddling in tents. Each evening, after tea, we were out somewhere, walking. On the first night, we marched off, up to the cliffs towards the lookout station, in a fiercely blowing wind. Someone peered out at us through the lookout window, and we were startled to see the face of Mr Evans inside, watching intently out to sea, all alone in the darkness. He welcomed us inside and told us a complicated story involving two ships, a cigarette end and his television set, which no doubt would have proved an epic and eerie ghost story – had we been able to follow it. But Mr Evans, a native Welsh speaker, speaks little English during the winter period, and we could hardly follow a word.

The next evening, we called on the local vicar and were welcomed by Mr Banks, not only warmly, but as if we were expected.

"How did you know we were here?" I asked.

Mr Banks said, "Well, I didn't exactly know, but I saw the tents and I wondered who in the world would camp here in midwinter, and I thought it must be you lot."

We didn't know whether to feel flattered. Mr Banks, however, was as delightful as ever, and his old dog, Whizzy, was still there with him, though now a little sleepy and arthritic. It was so nice to be in that familiar room once more, having the usual drink and chat. On the way home, I called in at the White Eagle to renew my acquaintance with the landlord and his Krupnik vodka.

On New Year's Eve, we walked up to the haunted farm, all hoping that the local ghost would show itself that night. Although the farm's surroundings were intensely lonely, nothing happened. But the next night, we went down to the beach, and something did happen: Harry and John Atkinson went swimming! The very sight of them took our breath away, at least as much as seeing a ghost. The rest of us admired their fortitude, but we refused to follow their lead. (Harry was subsequently revitalised and rewarded with a hot Krupnik at the White Eagle.)

Most of us spent the last evening in the farmhouse, over a cup of tea and a long chat with Mr and Mrs Evans. The conversation, predictably, was about strange happenings in and around Rhoscolyn, but once again, it proved difficult to follow. Mrs Evans, however, left us in no doubt of her opinion that the mothers of the young campers 'deserved a medal' for allowing their boys to come.

Even in the field, the dark evenings did nothing to dampen our spirits, nor our activities. We invented a mad game, which involved catching fugitives in torch beams. The fugitives, for their part, made nasty sorties and retreats on the torch bearers, from the cover of the undergrowth. Peter got the best laughs by mistaking a shallow pond for undergrowth and falling headlong into the cold water. Many evening hours were spent provoking Harry, with the young offenders being suitably chastised. We spent one morning exploring a deep valley and collecting driftwood, and another glorious afternoon on the cliffs. There were times when the winter sun felt so warm that we simply flopped on the heather and gazed up at the sky.

Wednesday, however, was cold, and most of the party went shopping in Holyhead. Peter, Michael and I disported ourselves in the field with an energetic form of golf, played with a mallet. It appeared that we came off better than the Holyhead party, who returned freezing cold. We had to tuck David Francis into bed to restore his circulation.

Despite the cold, we managed well in terms of food and sleep. Our theory involved not wasting daylight hours on cooking, but opting for a simple lunch, followed by a large cooked meal in the evening. The evening meals went as planned, but as the week bore on, the lunches simply got bigger and bigger. And as for sleep, the day didn't dawn until 9am, so there was little point in rising before 8.15am. To this practice, however, there was but one exception. On the first night, I awoke at 2.50am to the sound of a strange creature moving around in the field. It sounded like a large beast, which every so often, made a noise as if it were chewing a stick. I made a mental check on the list of British fauna to see if any large, nocturnal creature had any such habit. A beaver, perhaps? No, not a resident of the British Isles. Puzzled by the animal noises outside, I extracted myself from my sleeping bag and looked out into the moonlit field. The creature was, in fact, Harry.

"What," I asked courteously, "are you doing, Harry?"

"I'm lighting the fire," came the reply.

"You're just a little on the early side, no?"

"Why?" asked Harry. "It's 8.20am."

"No," I said. "It's 2.50am."

Harry looked at his watch again, this time closely, and said, "Ah yes!" and promptly returned to bed.

There were some lovely mornings that week. On New Year's Day, the Francis brothers were washing, shirtless, in the field, and Harry appeared in shorts. Then, we all went to the 10am service at Rhoscolyn Church and found it decked in all its Christmas finery, with Christmas tree, flowers and evergreens. As we emerged, we saw – as so often before – that panorama of coast, sea and rocks, with the Welsh mountains spread out before us in the sunshine.

There was one wet morning when Peter and I went shopping in Trearddur Bay, while Harry and Tony went off with an ambitious plan of spearing grouse. The alleged grouse, which must have been a rare aquatic variety, came to no harm, but the hunters returned somewhat worse for wear. Speaking of Tony reminds me that our one visitor was his father, who bravely drove down on New Year's Day. Mrs Layton, though laid low with the flu, had kindly sent a variety of food and comforts, which were most gratefully received.

Meanwhile, the dining shelter we had hired was never used for its intended purpose until the last morning, Saturday, when snow arrived. It was bad enough to cause a fatal crash at Valley Airport (we didn't hear of this until later). It did make us realise that winter camping could present certain difficulties.

It was a tough business dropping the tents, and there was the added anxiety whether our coach, due at 1.30pm, would succeed in getting through. To our surprise, it arrived perfectly on time. And then it was a matter of piling everything on board and wrapping ourselves in blankets before driving home through the lovely, snow-laden countryside. The woods of North Wales in their fresh covering of snow looked enchanting, and now, with our venture completed successfully, the weather could do what it liked.

We arrived home in a satisfied, even complacent, frame of mind. Among the major satisfactions was that, despite the prevailing epidemic, not one of our team had caught the flu or even a cold. Our open-air existence had stood us in good stead, even in midwinter. My other satisfaction was that everyone had coped so well. It was evident the present generation of young campers was at least as resourceful, hardy and competent as any of its predecessors.

# Chapter 5

When it appeared the number of campers in June 1970 would be rather small, my mind went back to a mobile camp in Galloway, some four years earlier. That party had enjoyed the experience of moving from place to place and had coped well with such a challenge. It seemed the right time to propose a similar experience to another generation of campers. There seemed no reason why it shouldn't be in Galloway once again.

We'd start at Wigtown, where Mrs Burnett – the mother of one our parishioners – kindly arranged a first site for us, which was to explore the area between the town and Luce Bay. We'd then make it our subsequent plan to reach the Mull of Galloway. The party mustered for this expedition included David Francis (who became our unofficial quartermaster), Tony Layton, Andrew Holt, Michael Daman, Stephen Francis, Ian Ray, and first-timers Glenn Wells and David Whitehead.

In early June that year, the weather was glorious. We enjoyed day after day of unbroken sunshine, with never a hint of rain. Such a day it was on the eve of our departure, and late that evening, I remember feeling the weather omens had never been so fair. The following morning, we set off at 8am by car for Manchester and were surprised to notice a few clouds gathering above. We thought little of it and caught our train to the north. We made changes at Preston and Carlisle, but emerged at Dumfries Station into pouring rain. This was such a shock that we didn't feel like facing it, so we hired a couple of taxis to take us to the bus station at Whitesands. A very acceptable and inexpensive lunch in an Indian restaurant prepared us for three hours in a bus, en route for Wigtown.

For an hour or more, we could see little but rain. However, at Kirkcudbright, bringing back memories of 1966, there was a squall. It looked like the front was passing, and so it turned out to be. Our progress westwards first brought a break in the clouds, then the end of the rain, and the sun was shining when, at last, we alighted in the broad square of the centre of Wigtown.

Mrs Burnett directed us to a site about a mile inland from the town, and we had hardly felt the weight of the packs on our backs before a kindly motorist offered to transport them down the road. It didn't disconcert him in the slightest that all the kit wouldn't fit in his car. He simply piled the rest on the bonnet and so conveyed them, and me, to our destination.

A ridge runs parallel with shore, just inland from Wigtown. We were just over the ridge in a small field, which we shared with a few beehives by the side of the local football pitch. It was well sheltered from the east (though not, as we later had cause to regret, from the west). There was water on hand and plenty of scrap timber lying around. Once we had beaten down the rather long grass, we soon had our four tents established, being watched, as we pitched them, by a curious and ever-increasing crowd of local boys and girls.

These visitors proved to be a regular feature of our time at Wigtown. The boys challenged us to a football match, while the girls were promised – by some – letters after we'd left (although I didn't observe that any were actually written). The local youngsters told us lurid tales of the fearsome youth of nearby Isle of Whithorn (see bottom photograph on page 94), where we had planned to go next. However, except for a handful of boys and girls in church, we saw no youngsters at all in the Isle of Whithorn. I don't know how long our curiosity value would have lasted at Wigtown, but it was maintained for at least a couple of days.

Our plan was to spend one full day at Wigtown. So, the following morning, Michael and I cooked, while the rest of the party went off exploring. We had a brief alarm when two women drove to the camp site, with an alarming report that our boys had been seen wandering on dangerous mudflats in front of Wigtown. Mike and I immediately went anxiously in search, but I suspect the element of danger had been somewhat exaggerated since we located the party back at the village, all wondering what the fuss had been about.

That afternoon, we took a bus ride to the Isle of Whithorn, which – of course – isn't an island at all, but is one of the most southerly villages and ports in Scotland. We had the idea of locating a site for a move the following day. It was a pleasant trip through that sleepy countryside. We liked the look of the Isle of Whithorn, and soon found a café serving the most excellent tea, scones and Scotch pancakes – which we subsequently visited several times after. Through the kindness of Mrs McWilliam at the quaint shop by the quayside, we were promised a site at her brother's farm at Cain Heads. So, all seemed set fair for our first move. But as we returned on the bus, the rain started, and it went on for almost 24 hours. The next morning was heavy with rain again, and as everything was soaked, we decided to put off our departure until the following day.

On going into the village that morning, we had the good fortune to run into David Whitehead's parents. They were on holiday, touring Scotland, and we were able to show them that, although David was wet through, he was none the worse for wear. By afternoon, the rain had cleared, and we decided to walk to Bladnoch with the aim of visiting both the local distillery and the creamery. But unfortunately, the distillery closes in the summer, and as we discovered, the creamery doesn't make cream. We were disappointed by our trip there, and when I tasted a dram of Bladnoch later that day in Wigtown, I felt disappointed by that too.

Meanwhile, Thursday was a good day. After a fine morning and an early lunch in Wigtown square, we all took the bus to the Isle of Whithorn. Mrs McWilliam directed us to Cairn Heads, 2.5 miles away. And once again, our burning shoulders were relieved, this time by a van driver who picked us up on the roadside and dropped us perfectly at the farm gate. Within minutes, the farmer was showing us to one of the finest sites we've ever seen.

Our field was huge, newly mown and stretched over a rounded headland. Bales of hay stood by the side in rows, three or four bales high. And the field itself was beautifully kept, with just a few swathes of hay lying round the edges. It would have been possible to pitch 1,000 tents in that field, and we had it all to ourselves. We selected a spot for our few tents where a dip in the land gave a suggestion of shelter from the west. The wall between the field and shore was enshrouded by honeysuckle. Wild roses and marsh orchid grew on the edges of the shore. I shall always associate Cairn Heads with the heady mix of hay and honeysuckle that, now in high summer, created a heavenly smell. From our tents, we looked out over the honeysuckle and the rocky shore to the broad waters of Creetown Bay, and beyond them to the receding hills of the Solway Coast. It was a most beautiful spot, and quiet too. During the four days of our stay there, we saw no one on, or from, the site, save the farmer and a couple of fishermen in a passing boat.

On our first evening, we walked to the tip of the headland, where the still-discernible traces of a Pictish fort could be seen. We wondered what scenes of blood and slaughter had been enacted there, centuries earlier. And we imagined, in that now peaceful spot, old Picts looking out fearfully across the sea for raiding Scots, or Vikings from faraway lands. As we walked back along the shore, we noticed relics from a more recent time of our country's peril. Smothered under roses and honeysuckle were the crumbling walls and cracking bases of what had been a few army huts from the last war. And then, nearer still to our tents, we saw emerging from the falling tide something even more remarkable. There was a ship stuck fast on the rocks, covered with barnacles. It was the strangest ship one could ever see. A superstructure seemed to be wholly lacking and about the hull there was a squareness that looked stranger still. We could make nothing of it.

The answer came the following morning when I met the farmer. He explained that, during the Second World War, Cairn Heads had been a training camp for troops and seamen who were to handle the Mulberry Harbours – temporary portable harbours to help with swift offloading of cargo. The wreck had been one of the many concrete-block ships that the men were learning to use before the Allied invasion of Normandy in the summer of 1944. It had been holed during a storm, and when the other concrete-block ships were towed off to France, that one had stayed put, remaining there for more than 25 years. It was stuck fast on the rocks, submerged by every rising tide and emerging again twice a day as the tide fell. The farmer told us of intense and secret activity that had gone on at Cairn Heads during those war years. Crowds of troops, along with senior officers, technicians, scientists and even politicians had held secret meetings there. He thought his farm would be ruined and its peace gone for ever. But now, a generation later, the soldiers had left, and nature had returned. All that remained of those hectic war years at Cairn Heads was that strange monument, a barnacle-covered ship, rising daily from the falling tide.

Next morning, we swam out to it. And at the expense of numerous scratches, we climbed aboard, but our exploration revealed nothing beyond what we could see from the shore.

We had intended to move on the Saturday, probably to Port William on the shore of Luce Bay, but the damp morning discouraged us from leaving our pleasant spot at Cairns Head. Instead, we decided to visit Port William by bus and return the same afternoon. We took a bus from the Isle to Whithorn and had a lengthy wait there before our connection to Port William. As we waited, Stephen's eye fell on a drinking fountain in the main street. He went over to the fountain and turned the handle for a drink, and just as he did, Whithorn's fire siren went off. Stephen's immediate thought was, *Goodness me...whatever have I done?* It was simply a remarkable coincidence. We discovered later that the siren's purpose was to alert the local firemen to come for their weekly practice.

By the time we reached Port William, a drizzle had started. Perhaps partly for that reason and partly as the tide was out – its wide, bare mudflats exposed – Port William seemed a rather grim little place. We ate our lunch by the quay, but what were we going do for the three hours or more until the bus returned? Here, our map stood us in good stead. For it showed a loch, known as the White Loch of Myrton, 1.5 miles from the village and set in the middle of a wood. It looked attractive, and a walk there would be better than simply hanging round the village. So off we went, meeting on the road the biggest herd of Friesian cows I've ever seen. As soon as we entered the woods, we realised we'd made a real find. The woods were delightful, open and grassy underfoot, but with a high cover of beech trees, shielding us entirely from any rain. There, in front of us, was the loch – bright and inviting against a dark background of trees. We could see why it was named the White Loch. Most of the party were set on swimming, and in that utterly quiet spot, a slight shortage of swimming trunks proved little inconvenience. So, an afternoon that had threatened to drag on proved all too short.

We discovered later from Mrs McWilliam that the woods and loch were private land, but the owner must have been a nice man, for Mrs McWilliam said, "I must tell him; he'll be so pleased to hear how much you enjoyed his woods."

Sunday was a quiet day. We went to church at the Isle of Whithorn to a service principally notable for the performance of the choir, comprising just one lady but with a voice so shrill as to be alarming. During the first hymn, she seemed to sense that her normal pre-eminence was being challenged by our five choristers. She gave us a look and then filled her lungs. Thereafter, we hadn't a chance. (We wished we'd had Bill Shore, our choirmaster, with us.) Also, that Sunday, David Whitehead was a little unwell, so we made him a bed of hay. Afterwards, he couldn't decide whether he was too ill to get up or simply too comfortable.

Sunday night was wild with rain and a westerly gale. Unfortunately, the dip where we'd pitched our tents turned out to be a wind tunnel. The small tents caught it the worst, especially since the soil was shallow and the brailing pegs not fully driven in. By morning, two were flattened, with the occupants lodging by now in the two larger tents. Several rips and holes had appeared, and a number sleeping bags were drenched. We were in a mess, and once more, there could be no question of moving.

When the rain eased, I asked David Francis and a few others to take the wet sleeping bags down to the Isle of Whithorn to see if some kindly soul would dry them for us. They trudged off, with their brightly coloured bundles, into the next field. I suppose it was these bundles that alarmed the cows, for they charged at our sorry party. I heard vivid accounts of how David had jumped the gate while retreating. I had to act as escort for everyone else going through that field for the rest of the day.

The post office lady, meanwhile, had volunteered to dry our sleeping bags, and later that day, a few local villagers became concerned about us, especially the café owners we'd come to know, following our frequent visits there. (On one occasion, a fisherman had given us a fine parcel of fresh caught plaice in that café.) But by teatime, all was well again. The small tents were beyond redemption, but we found that, with a squeeze, we could all fit into the large ones, which we re-pitched in the lee of the bales of hay.

Tuesday morning was glorious. I wakened earlier than necessary and sat for a long time at my tent door, watching hares and rabbits chase around the field. Obviously, if we were to reach the Mull of Galloway, we had to move that morning – so move we did. For once, no one gave us a lift, and with those heavy packs, the 2.5 miles to the village seemed a trek. But Ian, I remember, proved his stoutness of heart by cheerfully taking on extra weight. Then, from the Isle of Whithorn, we went off by bus through Wigtown, Newton Stewart and Stranraer, en route for Drummore, the last village on the Mull of Galloway. Alas, rain fell again, heavier and heavier, as we moved westwards. In Stranraer, we dripped into a café for tea, and then sheltered in the smart new railway terminal, where David Whitehead alarmed me by announcing he was seeing double (it proved to be tiredness). We had picked up our mail at Stranraer Post Office, and since we had received none so far, that was some consolation. But it was about the only consolation we had as we made the last stage of our journey to Drummore. The rain was heavy, the sky was dark and murky, and it was around 6pm. We still had no idea where we might camp or find shelter.

We needn't have worried. As we approached Drummore, the bus emptied, and the driver turned his attention to our problem. He told me of a farmer he knew who had a good barn. He suggested we dump our kit by the bus stop in Drummore and go at once to see him. So, we disembarked, and I was just explaining the plan, when a man came running through the rain from a shop opposite.

"Come inside," he waved, "and bring your kit in here. There's plenty of room in the shop."

Then, he got to work. He fetched the manager's wife first, and then the manager. After two minutes on the phone, the manager had found us a site by the shore at Low Coughie, and in another two minutes, he had the kit in his van. Another customer volunteered to take six of us in his car, and Michael, David and I were packed into the front seat of the little van. In no time at all, we were setting up camp again, and the rain started to peter out.

The wind change that Mike and I had thought we'd detected in the bus had, in fact, happened. The wind was now in the north, and there it remained for our couple of days at Drummore. It made things cooler, and we were driven to cooking and eating under canvas: how careful one had to be inside the tent! But our two large tents – well anchored with boulders from the store – stood up well, and we had no more trouble with rain.

Drummore, the last village on the promontory of Galloway, has that atmosphere of being 'at the end of the line', almost with the feel of an island. No one goes through Drummore; the only reason for being there is that one wants to be there. No one is in a hurry, and everyone's friendly. I suppose the highlights of our stay were, first, a football match against the Drummore boys (which despite the antics of a light ball in high wind, we contrived to win), and on the Wednesday evening, a trip by minibus to the lighthouse at the extremity of the Mull of Galloway. The wind was particularly strong and cold that evening, but at the end of the journey, we managed to get far enough down the cliff to be sheltered from the north. We sat there for a long time, watching seabirds soaring, wheeling and diving about the cliffs. Among them were gannets, and I was pleased to see the breed after so many years of searching for them in vain along our western coasts.

It was satisfying to have reached our destination, and I remember how jolly and good-tempered our little party was during those last couple of days at Drummore. A game was, again, invented on the site, which involved sending cockle shells soaring in the wind, frequently aimed at me as a final target. We had a quiz on the last evening. With such harmless activities, along with strolls into the village, the two days passed pleasantly enough. In the main pub of the village, I had the unusual experience of being bought more drinks by the barman – a schoolteacher by profession and a church organist as a sideline – than I bought for him, myself or anyone else. Glen Grant was my drink there.

On the morning of our departure, everything was so utterly quiet that it seemed improbable that any traffic, let alone our bus, would appear. But it did so around 7.45am, and we had a pleasant, sleepy drive in the sunshine through Port Logan and up the mull to Stranraer. There, we were lucky to find a café, which served us an excellent breakfast of bacon sandwiches. Soon after, we were off on the long, four-hour bus ride to Dumfries. What a quiet journey that was, even though it was mid-morning. The midsummer traffic was so slight that we began timing the intervals between vehicles passing us in the opposite direction. There was one interval of 5 minutes, and several of 2 or 2.5 minutes, and that was on Galloway's main artery from Stranraer to Dumfries. I enjoyed that leisurely drive and quite regretted its end at Dumfries. From there, we took a quiet, uneventful train ride home.

In Boswell's Journal of a *Tour to the Hebrides with Samuel Johnson, LL.D 1773*, James Boswell writes "The incidents upon a journey are remembered with particular pleasure."[10] It has certainly been a pleasure to recall the incidents of this journey through Galloway. I wish I could recall as well the incessant flow of jokes, puns and witticisms from Andy Holt that accompanied our journey and entertained us all. Andy's wit is of an airy, bubbly quality: it flits and floats away before you can fasten it onto the tablets of memory. But one of his shafts of brilliance did leave its mark. We were discussing at the Isle of Whithorn whether Harold Wilson, having ceased to be Prime Minister, would continue to be a Right Honourable.

"Yes," I said. "He'll still be a member of the Privy Council, so he'll still have the title of Right Hon."

Keeping discreetly out of range, Andy quipped, "If our vicar ever got a title, it wouldn't be a Right Hon. He'd be a Write Off."

# Chapter 6

Many times over the last 20 years, I've had the impression that our last camp has been our best. I'm ready to admit that this impression has often been an illusion, but at the present moment, I'd claim it isn't an illusion and our camp in August 1970, although small in numbers, was the most varied, the most interesting, the most enjoyable, and if I dare use the term, the most *educational* of our entire series of camps.

The company, first of all, was Michael Daman, David Francis, Tony Layton, Ian Ray, Stephen Andrews and Ian Aitchison. This bunch had an average of rather more than five camps apiece behind them. The plan was to repeat 'somewhere north of Glasgow' such a wandering life as we had enjoyed in Galloway in June. We had, when we left home, no definite goal for our journey, and could give to parents only the vague suggestion that, if they addressed mail to the post office at Mallaig, we might just receive it. However, we did have a bible for our wanderings, which was that splendid volume published by the Highlands and Islands Development Board containing timetables of every bus, train, boat and plane in the north and west of Scotland. So many times consulted, that guide proved a good friend. Only once, at Acharacle, did it let us down.

Mr Daman and Mr Layton took us once more to Manchester Victoria station, and late-morning on a sunny Monday, we arrived at Glasgow Central Station just before noon. En route, we had checked out the bus service north of Glasgow and found we could be in Glencoe by 8.30pm that evening. Since the weather was promising, that seemed a reasonable objective. Our first task in Glasgow was to find the terminus of the Oban bus. We ran it to earth near Glasgow Queen Street station, thankfully dumped our packs, and then found a substantial lunch in a Fuller's Café. Shopping followed, and we thought it prudent to be fully stocked for at least two days. Other minds, especially David's, proved sharper than mine in remembering all we'd need. It was a considerable bulk of goods that we carried back to the bus station.

Around 4.30pm, a bus arrived, taking on a full load of passengers. Ian Aitchison and I got seats behind a gentleman in full Highland dress of the Campbell tartan (as he soon informed us). He was a friendly, enthusiastic Scot and also a tireless purveyor of information. Our difficulty was that, as well as his strong Scottish accent, he possessed a slight speech impediment, and so his information often remained a mystery. Every two minutes or so, I had to lean forwards to unravel some excited information the gentleman was tossing over his shoulder. When unravelled, the information wasn't always sensational: "That's the River Clyde; ships come up it to Glasgow," or, "Yon's the banks of Loch Lomond. There's a song about them," and, "Ye might see some deer on the mountains."

Ian gave up the struggle and promptly went to sleep. Michael, meanwhile, was having a long conversation with a Scottish Venture Scout, while others enjoyed the splendid scenery as we skirted Loch Long and the upper reaches of Loch Lomond, before the steady pull up to Crianlarich.

There, to my distinct relief, we changed to the Fort William bus. And like so many buses we took in the next few days, it was virtually empty except for us. I asked the driver whether there was open land in Glencoe where we could pitch our three tents.

"Och aye!" he said. "Ye'll want to be put off there, before we get down into the village."

I agreed, sitting back, and exchanged comments with Michael on the sweeping hills of Glen Orchy, and the ribbons of road and railway traversing it, along with the toy-like stations and glimpses of the great Rannoch Moor.

Eventually, the road swung westwards. The sun was shining, but patches of cumulus were drifting in from the west. They seemed to gather and lower as the eastern rim of the Pass of Glencoe opened up to us. It was an impressive drive into and down the pass. Huge hills towered, brooding on either side of the valley. We passed rushing burns and torrents, all grim associations of that infamous place.

There were a number of tents pitched on grassy hillocks, and on the edge of streams, several vacant spots would have been ideal for our site. But the driver didn't stop, and we took it that there were still better spots further down the pass. He had either forgotten or misunderstood our wishes. We realised that we'd left the pass with the best sites now two or three miles back. By then, we were already down in the village. It was a pity. I looked for a minibus or cabs to take us back up the pass, but nothing was available. In the village itself, there were no camp sites, and it was now 8.30pm with darkness closing in. The only thing to do was to walk back up the pass and trust we'd find a convenient spot before darkness fell or our shoulders simply grew too weary. It proved a tough walk, carting that fair old weight of supplies, as well as our own packs. We pressed on for a couple of miles until the roadside verge opened into a strip just wide enough for our tents. We quickly pitched the tents with their rears to the road, made do with biscuits and a piece of cake for supper, and were soon in bed. Rochdale already seemed thousands of miles away.

There would be a bus leaving Glencoe at 8.15am the following morning, so we decided to catch that, cross Loch Linnhe by ferry from Ardgour, and make for Morvern and the southern end of Loch Shiel. That morning, David found a handy burn for a wash and a drink. We set up our stoves on the edge of the road and made breakfast. Then, the bus came, and we were away, down the pass and through the village, with the bus stopping for the driver to deliver milk, mail or papers, or just to have a chat. We enjoyed a great scenic drive along the south shore of Loch Leven, changed buses at Kinlochleven, and then boarded a crowded bus going westwards along the north shore of the loch, through North Ballachulish, to the ferry at Ardgour. The quaint little ferry was waiting for the bus passengers, and we were soon across the water. It was here where we then started to feel the remoteness of this territory west of Loch Linnhe.

Another fine ride followed alongside Loch Sunart, through Strontian (a tiny village from which the world famous and sinister element Strontium 90 takes its name) and Salen, to the crofting village of Acharacle. We scanned around for a site and stopped the bus beside a small, round *lochan*, half-covered with water lilies. And we found just enough space for our tents on the edge of that tiny lake, among the heather and rough grass.

After tea, we had a long walk westwards on a nearby track. While passing through another little crofting community, we were able to see what crofting was really like, noticing the tiny size of some of the crofts and the poverty of the dwellers living there. Peat smoke came from a little cottage with a corrugated-iron roof. The crofter's wife, in a rough hessian apron, was talking to her husband in Gaelic, spoken now by little over one percent of the population of Scotland. The day ended with most of the party, but not me, scaling the hill that overlooked our site and Acharacle.

The next day, our plan was to move north to Lochailort by bus, where we should be back on the road and railway line leading to Morar and Mallaig. But we received a wide variety of opinions from locals and our timetable guide on whether a bus actually went to Lochailort from Acharacle. So, we walked into the village the following morning to check the facts. Even there, I was given four different perspectives on the journey, which were the following:

1.  a bus would take us to Lochailort at 4pm that afternoon;
2.  if we walked seven miles to Kinlochmoidart, we'd be able to catch a bus to Lochailort;
3.  the bus would take us to Kinlochmoidart, from where we'd have a seven-mile walk to Lochailort; and
4.  no bus went anywhere in that direction, at all.

Perplexed by all this, I then luckily spotted a poster in a shop window advertising daily sailings on Loch Shiel to Glenfinnan. There was a boat, apparently, which was due to leave in a couple of hours. Well, Glenfinnan would suit us just as well as Lochailort, wouldn't it? So, we formulated a quick change of plan. It was swiftly back to the *lochan* to dismantle and collect our tents, organise a quick picnic by the roadside, and then scuttle down to the little pier where a boat would be waiting to take us the 18 miles down Loch Shiel to Glenfinnan.

There was only one other passenger, a French student, and unless we were misled by his indifferent English – and our worse French – he was travelling around Scotland with no more kit than would fit in his pockets, and sleeping, as he put it, "under the open air".

It was a superb sail down that lonely, beautiful loch. On one side, there isn't a single habitation; on the other, there's just one, and that was empty. As we approached the north end of the loch, we saw the famous monument to the '45 Rebellion (the Jacobite uprising of 1745), which towered there, right in front of us.

We also saw clouds lowering, and rain started to fall. Several wet hours ensued. There wasn't a soul in sight at Glenfinnan Pier. We made vain forays in a couple of directions in search of a site, and Stephen even volunteered to get into his trunks and cross a considerable burn on the far side to where the ground seemed better. On closer inspection, however, Stephen judged the ground unsuitable; it was as well that he did. In a couple of hours, that burn had swelled to a raging torrent. Had we camped across there, we could have been stuck for days. Eventually, David found a wide, grassy corner on the edge of a wood, where the ground was level enough to take our tents. We were thankful to get inside, away from the heavy rain. More thankful still, we were, when we dried off and enjoyed a hot meal. After supper, Stephen and Ian Ray decided to go swimming in Loch Shiel in the rain. They were as good as their word and claimed, of course, the loch to be warm.

I don't wish to revive unpleasant memories here, but I ought to mention our visitors at Glenfinnan – the midges. They plagued us all evening and the following morning. It was inevitable, I suppose, in such a sheltered, wooded spot with wet, windless weather. Partly to escape the infuriating midges and partly in the hope of less cloud and rain near the coast, we decided to move on the next day to Arisaig. There would be a train around 1.30pm, but much earlier than this, we carried our first load of kit up the steep hill to the station with the hope of finding shelter, both from the rain and, worse, the midges. Our hopes were more than fulfilled. Without being asked, the stationmaster put one of the waiting rooms at our disposal, complete with antique stove and as much coal as we wanted. Tony lit a fire while the rest of us went for a second load of kit. I bought some crisps from a nearby pub (there was no shop within miles), and we had a midge-free meal, a good drying out and a long quiz before the train arrived. (See photograph on page 95.)

We hadn't travelled very far west when the sky brightened and the prospect of sunshine appeared over the coast. We all felt great until I realised I'd left my anorak at Glenfinnan station. The anorak didn't matter that much, but what did matter was that it had all the camp money in one of the pockets. We held a hasty conference in the guard's van, added up what money we had between us, decided we had enough to buy food until morning and promptly stopped worrying. In fact, I was reunited with my anorak just a few hours later, when it was sent on the next train.

After shopping and exploring Arisaig, we then settled on a site we called Tree Tops. Separated from the shore by a narrow road, a wooded hillside rises to the south of Arisaig. Some 30 feet above the road, we found a spot where, with a little ingenuity in fixing guy lines to branches, we could accommodate our three tents. From there, simply by pushing away a few branches, we were rewarded with a superb view over the sea, with the Isle of Eigg ahead and the Isle of Skye to the right. It wasn't what I'd call a *convenient* site, but it was certainly a dramatic one, and our first evening there was quite memorable. We decided to have a rest the following day and postpone moving on until Saturday.

Tony had earlier spoken with some people at Acharacle, who said if we were ever near Arisaig, we should visit the fine beach of silver sand at Rhue. We decided to make a visit there our main activity of the day. We spent a leisurely morning wandering round Arisaig, lunched at our campsite and then set out on the walk, alleged to be four miles each way. We agreed afterwards that it was at least six miles – a good walk on a sunny afternoon – ending successfully at the beach in question. It certainly was a pleasant, silvery beach, and most of us had an enjoyable swim. But having seen the great silver beaches of Islay and Coll, we weren't as enthusiastic about it as Tony's informants. Nor were we that impressed, in the next few days, by the White Sands of Morar. I suppose, by now, we were getting rather choosy and somewhat sophisticated as travellers throughout the Western Isles.

That evening, the midges struck again; this time, murderously. In the hope of escaping them, we cooked our meal on the road, but all was in vain. They were everywhere. We were driven to walking quickly up and down the road as we ate. We attempted but failed to outdistance our pursuers, which started to spread themselves, lightly but infuriatingly, on our plates of food. A few people passing in cars, who were unaware of the midges, gave us very strange looks. We must have looked possessed. Many wore pyjamas, covering and protecting their entire bodies, while others had towels over their heads. Strange sights to behold. And after the midges came the heavy rain. It was with us all night! This was the only time we got a sleeping bag wet during the camp. It was still heavy by morning. Conditions were stacking against our plan of simply packing up and moving on, as intended, to Morar or Mallaig. Instead, we decided to go to Mallaig, just for the day, and return at teatime.

We weren't the only wet people in Mallaig that day. The little port was full of them: bearded climbers on their way to or from Skye, families from the camping sites round Morar, and one soaked group of students who had just returned from Eigg. It was just too wet to do much but pick up our mail and kill time in shops and cafés. At least we got a good lunch – for my part, an excellent piece of salmon – and we had an adequate tea in a café. In a splendid little fish shop, we bought large prawns and small haddies, which stood us in good stead that evening and the following morning. Then, it was back to Arisaig by bus, stopping en route to help push a car out of a ditch. (Ian Aitchison was behind a wheel when it started and got himself a mud bath.)

We were all soaked by then and didn't fancy the idea of returning to that dripping site for the night. It seemed the right time to have a word with Mr Urquhart, the minister whom we had already met. We called at the manse and asked him if he knew of any barns or perhaps a bothy where we might spend the night. Mrs Urquhart was called and a conference ensued: she was voluble; he was reflective. Eventually, their ideas converged. Why not stay in the vestry that joined the manse to the church? Why not, indeed? In minutes, the Urquharts were fetching an electric fire, moving furniture and offering us hot water. They were so generous, thoughtful and kind. Soon, we had brought our essential kit from the tents. We got our stoves going on the floor of the vestry and made a meal including those delicious prawns. We had that wonderful feeling that comes of being warm, dry and fed, following a rough, wet day in the great outdoors. Is there any pleasure like that?

Around 9am, Mr Urquhart came through the vestry to prepare the church for morning service. We told him we'd be attending and asked if he'd like us to go through the hymns. We went into church and, with Mr Urquhart on the organ, held a good choir practice. It must be unique in the long annals of choir practices in that several choristers were actually wearing pyjamas.

Cooking haddies must also be a rarity in church vestries, but it happened on the Sunday morning. We had all smells and mess cleared away in good time for the service. In church, which had a pretty large congregation, we were put on the front row as choristers, and the minister gave a public welcome to "members of the Sigma organisation". It was a fine service. I remember that, afterwards, we had tinned ham for lunch, and Mrs Urquhart brought us a jar of tomato chutney to go with it, as good as any Mr Daman makes. In the afternoon, we did no more than stroll a mile or so along the road to Morar.

We were tired by this stage of the camp, and that leisurely day in the vestry had done us all good. It was still wet until teatime, but afterwards, things began to look up. I discussed with Mike whether, despite our long stay at Arisaig, it would still be possible to reach Eigg, which had seemed an appropriate goal for our journey. We decided that if the weather allowed us to make an early start in the morning, we'd be able manage it. Without further ado, we walked back to site and packed, ready for morning.

As Mike and I lugged those heavy tents back to the manse, I had a growing feeling that our troubles were over and easier days lay ahead. The wind, which had been slowly veering since morning, was now distinctly north, rather than west. The cloud was rising slowly but steadily, and there were traces of bright and dry, if coolish, weather ahead. I remember feeling contented as we trudged along the shore that Sunday evening.

I wasn't to be disappointed. There came a lovely morning, and after the good rest, we were as bright as the morning and all ready for the port of Mallaig and, thereafter, the Isle of Eigg. We left the Urquharts with words of thanks and set off by train to Mallaig, which was as cheerful on the Monday as it had been gloomy on the Saturday. We had much to do, including plenty of shopping, checking on the sailing times, and making arrangements regarding mail and money. We'd also have to organise a meal before the boat left at 1.30pm. Our original idea was to have just one night on Eigg, crossing on the mail boat on the Monday afternoon and returning on a pleasure boat on Tuesday evening. To this end, we did our budgeting and arranging, and then went to the familiar café for lunch.

As we sat down to lunch, however, I began to have second thoughts. It seemed a shame to have only one night on Eigg, and in any case, with the breeze strong and the sea choppy, the pleasure boat might not even sail on the Tuesday. Could we pinch an extra day on Eigg, return on the mail boat on Wednesday and still be home by Thursday night? A quick check on the timetables revealed that it was possible. What about the cash I had to obtain on Wednesday morning at Mallaig Post Office?

Provided British Rail would take a cheque for our tickets home, we could manage without the money. A quick discussion needed a quick decision. But should we risk a change of plan? A unanimous "Yes!" from our group led me to setting my soup aside, before dashing to the station. I asked if British Rail would accept a cheque, which they agreed to do. I then ran to the ferry office and cancelled our passage on the pleasure boat.

"Ye're verra wise," said the girl behind the counter. "She probably wouldn't be sailing anyway."

I swallowed a glass of Glenfarclas 105 proof to celebrate our change of plan, dashed back to the café and caught up with the others on their main course.

Then, it was down to the quay to catch the mail boat. We helped to load it – mail, passengers' luggage, bread, beer and tractor parts, all on together. They were sorted only into their four possible destinations, which were Eigg, Muck, Rhum and Canna. It was an excellent sail of about 90 minutes to Eigg, albeit a little choppy after leaving the lee of Skye, when some queasiness ensued. But it was calmer once we were again in the lee of Eigg, and we were all in good form when the boat hove to off the island, and a ferry boat appeared to carry us ashore.

I noticed two incidents that tell a great deal about Scots in general, and islanders in particular. As well as the little ferry, there came to meet our boat one of those rubber dinghies with an outboard motor. It was piloted by a smart-looking man, who turned out to be a rather well-known journalist.

He waved at and called out urgently to one of our ship's crew who was beside me, busy with a rope: "Have you got that petrol for me? I'm waiting for it."

The sailor hesitated. "Nae," he said. "It's no on the ship today."

The man in the dinghy veered away in a bad temper and a cloud of spray.

The sailor muttered to me: "We've got it all right, but yon fella's a wee bit impatient."

Two days later, when we boarded the boat on our return, I noticed that the crew let the man have his petrol.

Also on the boat to Eigg was a large man, overly dressed for the circumstances, who looked displeased with the company he was having to keep. I would have described him as 'aloof', but the boys had already nicknamed him 'Lord Muck'. When it came time for his smart luggage to be handed down into the ferry boat, he made imperious remarks about "being careful with it all". No one said anything, but I could swear his luggage ended up in the wettest, grubbiest corners of the ferry, after being dropped, thrown and turned upside down a remarkable number of times. By contrast, our shabby kit was carefully, almost tenderly, handled. I shall long remember that.

We had hardly got on the ferry before I was in conversation with a man who had come out on it from the island. He turned out to be a priest – Father Barrett-Lennard from the Brompton Oratory in London – who had for years been coming to Eigg for holidays. While on holiday, he'd take the service in the Roman Catholic church on the island. He proved to be a good and helpful friend. First came his suggestion for a site at the Bay of Laig (see photograph on page 96) on the far side of the island, near the church.

When we had landed and wondered how to cover the five or six miles to the site, he said: "Just put your kit on that old cart behind that tractor."

We did as he said, and then helped to load another cart with bread, mail and orange crush. We then simply sat on our cart among all our kit.

After a few minutes, a man came up, asked courteously where we were going, and then said, "Are you all ready?"

We nodded, and he jumped on the tractor and drove up the road with our gang bumping and rattling in the old cart behind.

After a couple of miles, however, we came to an abrupt stop at a dilapidated building of corrugated iron. It was the island's one and only shop. Another tractor in front of us pulled up, and an old banger of a car, coming from the other direction, stopped too. The postman rode up on his bike, with the mail in a rucksack on his back, and he jumped off. Everything and everyone stopped. Passing Eigg's only shop without stopping was clearly unthinkable on the island. Some people went into the shop, while others stood around outside, exchanging pleasantries. Most of the men bought a can of beer in the shop, drank it by the roadside, and threw the empty onto an enormous pile of cans by the side of the shop. Everyone had a good old chat – mostly, it appeared, in Gaelic. After about 15 minutes, the gathering broke up just as casually and spontaneously as it had come together. They all nodded at each other and then went their various ways. Strictly speaking, they had only two ways to choose from – the way we were going or the opposite direction – as there's only one road on Eigg of about five miles long.

We jolted on, presuming our driver knew where we wanted to go. He evidently did, because as we came over the ridge of the island and saw the road winding down to the western coast, he pointed out a magnificent sweep of silver sand and shouted to me, *"Yon's the Bay of Laig."*

Ten minutes later, we were unloading our kit on the *machir* grass at the edge of the bay.

And what a site that was! Of all the campsites we've known over many, many years, none could make so perfect a subject for the artist's brush. Plumb in front of us, across seven miles of sea, the majestic mountains of Rhum rose out of the water. Behind us, gently enfolding our site, was an enormous amphitheatre of cliffs, which were 1,000 feet high. And at our feet, a beach of silver sand lay flawless and untrodden, stretching 1,000 yards in either direction. The smoke from a dozen crofts drifted up above the little pasture between the cliffs and the shore. And during the time of our stay, the blue sky was broken only by the odd cumulus cloud, appearing like a puff of smoke above the cliffs behind us or marooned on the mountains of Rhum. It was so very beautiful, and for a short time, belonged only to us.

Tony made tea, and apart from a bit of triple-jumping on the sand, we didn't do much that evening. It was enough to sit, look and listen.

Around sunset, our friend the priest appeared for cocoa and a chat. I asked if he'd take our evening prayers. He readily agreed and invited us to say them with him in the tiny Catholic church that stood some 100 yards back from the shore. We strolled up there, two candles were lit in the church, and our good friend said prayers. At the end of prayers, our voices joined in 'God, That Madest Earth and Heaven'. The singing of that hymn, left to our five choristers, always brings me back to that moment, that place.

Afterwards, Father Barrett-Lennard asked quietly if I'd do him a great favour. Could I persuade one or two of the boys to sing the following evening at a Mass in a croft for an old woman who was very ill. "Perhaps half a dozen of the crofters will be coming to the Mass," said Father Barrett-Lennard. "And, you see, they never hear any proper singing here, since there's no one who can sing."

No persuasion was needed.

Next evening, we all walked in the sunshine to that croft and were gravely ushered in to join half a dozen men and women in the neat front room. Although the service wasn't our own, we felt very much at one with that little company of islanders. We felt as if we belonged together. Having no hymn books, we sang from memory 'The King of Love', 'Wherefore, O Father' and 'Praise to the Holiest' – three hymns our two churches have in common. When the service ended, I was shown into the bedroom of the frail old woman for whose sake these things had been arranged. She thanked me and all of us, not effusively or sentimentally, but with a restrained and reverent courtesy that deeply impressed me.

That experience was part of a very memorable day. In the morning, we went to the shop – that's to say, we had a five-mile walk over land as quiet and as beautiful as you can find anywhere in Britain – so as to do the shopping. I remember how vividly beautiful the heather was. I wished so much that we had more time to enjoy and explore this place. After lunch, we managed a bit more exploration. We had heard of a beach of 'singing sands' a couple of miles to the north. We scrambled along the shore through an area of eroded rocks and huge, shallow pools that looked like a miniature Arizona – a strange and impressive stretch of shoreline. On reaching the sands, we could hear their singing, or at least we could hear a kind of squeaking. We returned along the cliff top, which involved a different kind of walk, but an equally enjoyable one. I found some good flowers, including field gentian. Then came tea, followed by the service in the croft. After the service, most of us went for an evening swim – which even included Mike (that, in itself, made it a red-letter day). A wonderfully full day ended with another visit from Father Barrett-Lennard, who entertained us with a long and complicated ghost story.

Then came the day for us to leave Eigg. Mike and I started with an early, long walk to locate the man with the tractor, who agreed to fetch us by mid-morning. On time, we trundled back across the island, stopping off en route, of course, at the shop. We then headed down to the quay, where we lit up our stoves and prepared corned beef hash and rice pudding for lunch. We knew it would be our last hot meal for some time. We missed out on our coffee, as the boatmen decided they couldn't get the ferry up to the quay, so they had to take us and our kit out to the boat by dinghy, in relays. To board the dinghy, we had to climb down the side of the quay on a rope. I recall wondering how an elderly person would have been able to leave Eigg on that day. We transferred from the ferry on to the mail boat and enjoyed an excellent cruise through the Small Isles – calling at Muck, Rhum and Canna – on that lovely afternoon. The total fare for our sail out to Eigg, plus our six-hour return journey, was 12 shillings and 6 pence for me (around 62p in today's money) and exactly half that for each of the boys.

I had a long chat on the boat with an army colonel and his wife, on birds of the islands, as well as on writers on the Hebrides. Towards sunset, Mallaig came up on the starboard bow. People began to ask me what we'd be doing for the night, and one helpful soul promised to run me out in his car to find a site near Mallaig, and then come back afterwards for the others. We were glad of that: it was getting chilly, with a breeze now freshening out of that blood-red sky. The water around Mallaig Pier was also high and choppy. And somehow, it wasn't surprising that a series of dramatic events started to unfold before us. First, our boat hit the pier, not dangerously but hard enough to startle us. As we drew breath, there were screams from the end of the pier. A boy had fallen into the boisterous sea. People moved swiftly, as did a fishing smack moored next to us. I saw a man race down the quay and dive in with never a pause. We heard later that both he and the boy had been rescued. As we disembarked, a car raced down the quay to the first accident and, right in front of us, knocked down a child. More screams here, but fortunately, this victim came to little harm. I told our party, rather tensely, to be careful.

But all was well. The kind friend with the car soon delivered us to a patch of roadside grass, less than 600 yards from the centre of Mallaig. Our tents went up with the speed that comes of much practice. And within 45 minutes of our landing at Mallaig, I was back in the village, making a phone call home. David organised a quick supper, and we were soon all to bed.

In the morning, we were up before 6am, and we dropped the tents and packed in no time. We were down at the station in plenty of time for the train, which was due to leave at 7am. Coffee was being brewed on the platform when I arrived with the tickets, and welcome it was. And then, on that day-long but interesting journey home, we made sandwiches in a rather crude but effective way. We dozed on and off, and I had a long talk with a shepherd. We saw Arisaig and Glenfinnan again, and we got off for a stretch and a cup of coffee at Fort William. Mike spent hours examining every detail of Rannoch Moor, and we talked about many, many things before dozing off again. We changed, of course, at Glasgow, and Tony made a kind speech in the station at Glasgow Central. He presented me with a kind gift from the party, which is much treasured but little deserved. And as we got near to Manchester, of course it started to rain. We all talked, more and more animatedly, about the huge, hot meal we were planning to have back home. I got one, and trust everyone else did too.

All had gone well once more. And as I lay down my pen (or rather rest my typing finger) at the end of this series of reminiscences, I do so with a sense of gratefulness that, down the years, all has gone so well. Accidents have been slight, illnesses rare and hard words so few on all our expeditions. Laughs have been many, tempers controlled and kindness so natural. And if any reader has got as far as this, he may well count the blessings of his many camping holidays. If he does, then however large his total of blessings, I can assure him that mine is a great deal larger still.

*From top left: Choirboys on a wet Whitsun walk in Kirkholt, Rochdale, in 1966 (with the editor at the rear). In its late 1960s heyday, the choir had around 35 choristers. Top right: Canon Vanstone on an Easter walk on the estate where he worked as parish vicar. Bottom centre: Despite numerous offers of top academic posts, Vanstone was entirely committed to his parishioners.*

Top: *The whisky distillery of Laphroaig on the Isle of Islay. Along with Glenfarclas 105, Laphroaig was one of Vanstone's favourite single malts, which he'd enjoy with a Capstan (full strength) cigarette. Bottom: The gorgeous bay of Tobermoray on the Isle of Mull, with its colourful row of seafront buildings; this is often the first port of call after Oban, while en route to the Inner Hebrides.*

*Top: The Coll Hotel and a Church of Scotland overlook the peaceful harbour at the village of Arinagour, Isle of Coll, one of the Hebridean islands Vanstone's campers returned to on several occasions. Bottom: Tourists are ferried back to Fionnphort on the south-west of the Isle of Mull, after a day trip to Staffa. Iona Abbey, in the background, was the birthplace of Christianity in Scotland – and later, England – after Irish monk Columba brought the new religion to Iona from Ireland in 563.*

*Hexagonal basalt columns at Fingal's Cave, Staffa (made famous in* The Hebrides *[overture] by Mendelssohn). Many of the Hebridean campers were also choristers at St Thomas' Church, Kirkholt (inset). According to 'Sir', their voices, on that day, "soared above the crash of waves and lingered high in the lofty dome of the cave".*

Top: Puffins on the uninhabited island of Staffa in the Inner Hebrides keep guard after catching a mouthful of fish. Spotting puffins, seals and basking sharks became a camp favourite, along with endless cricket on makeshift machir pitches or swimming in the cool waters of the Atlantic. Bottom: A single young sailor rows out into the bay at the village of the Isle of Whithorn – which isn't an island at all, but is one of the most southerly seaports in Galloway, south-west Scotland. It was also the location of one of many Scottish camping tours (this one in June 1970) led by Canon Vanstone.

*Steam engine (No. 45231) pulls carriages over the famous Glenfinnan Viaduct en route to Mallaig, a regular starting point for Canon Vanstone's tours to the Western Isles in the late 1960s and early 1970s.*

*Dramatic cliffs overlook the tiny hamlet of Cleadale, near the campsite at the Bay of Laig on the Isle of Eigg's western coastline. Vanstone's young campers endlessly searched the coastline here for driftwood, which was used for cooking.*

Top: Oban by night. This western-seaboard Scottish port was the springboard for numerous camping tours for the boys of St Thomas' Church, Kirkholt, Rochdale. Vanstone's character-building camps affected those boys (now men in advanced middle age) in more ways than they could ever have realised. Bottom: One of the hardy, diminutive, wild Shetland ponies by the side of Loch Sgioport, South Uist. The rugged beauty of those landscapes through which Vanstone and his camping 'colleagues' travelled stayed with them for decades.

*Highland cattle paddle in front of Breachacha Castle in the south of the Isle of Coll in the Inner Hebrides. The castle, which is six miles from camp, would often prove a useful destination point for a 'quick' walk.*

*Top: Sunset at Baleloch, in North Uist, the Outer Hebrides. One of the tours that surprised Canon Vanstone for "getting as far as we did". He added, "We travelled on trust, arriving at each destination, more or less, when intended." The August 1971 tour with 12 teenagers from a Rochdale council estate included the Isle of Coll, Barra, South Uist, Benbecula, North Uist, the Isle of Skye and Mallaig. Bottom: Neist Point, the Isle of Skye's most westerly location, is home to one of the most famous lighthouses in Scotland. For Vanstone, the west represented "the land of the sunset, the land of affectionate longing and gentle regret".*

*Top: Impressive sweep of land and sea at Machrins Bay on the west coast of the Isle of Colonsay – a favourite site for Canon Vanstone and his team of Hebridean explorers. Bottom: The majestic sweep of Kiloran Bay, Isle of Colonsay – one of the most staggeringly beautiful sites visited by Bill Vanstone and his team during his 20-year period of camping in "the realms of gold". Inset: The editor (centre), aged 16, at Kiloran Bay in August 1973, with two of his camping 'colleagues' – Ian Aitchison (left) and Stephen Andrews (right). "The finest bay I have ever seen in my life," Tony Layton said at the time. Canon Vanstone later wrote: "The beach lay there in front of us, about 0.75 miles long, with sand of rich gold, and water combining all the richest blues one can imagine – cobalt, turquoise and ultramarine."*

*Top: Canon Bill Vanstone was described by* The Independent *as – "The most intellectually brilliant of the many able men ordained after the Second World War." Bottom: Editor and author together – Tony Layton, editor of* Hebridean Odysseys, *with theologian and author, Canon Vanstone at the National Arboretum, Gloucestershire, in 1998, the year before 'our vicar' died.*

# PART 2

Round Many Western Isles

# Chapter 7

Looking back, I'm surprised that, during our tour of the Hebrides in 1971, we got as far as we did. There's something about the Hebrides – be it the vagaries of the boat service, the allurements of certain islands or just the timelessness of island life – which diverts travellers from their original destination. It leaves them becalmed but content on some unexpected shore. One meets, for example, on the Isle of Coll a holidaymaker who intended to sail out to Barra, but who remained enchanted by Coll; on Barra, a couple there because they missed the ferry to South Uist; or on the Isle of Eigg, a traveller who didn't know there's only one boat a week to Muck. On the other hand, we performed fairly exactly our original intention of sailing via Coll to the outer islands, before returning through the Isle of Skye to Mallaig.

This was partly due to luck and partly to trust. We had learned from experience that MacBrayne's steamers, however long delayed, do eventually arrive. Meanwhile, on land, although buses may be unheard of in certain areas, there's always someone who has a dump truck, an ancient minibus or a dilapidated tractor pulling an even more dilapidated trailer. To trust that one will find such a conveyance must be added to the yet braver sense that, when found, it will actually work. But surprisingly, it often does. Travelling on trust, we arrived at each successive destination, more or less, when we had intended.

Our first destination, and the only prearranged one, was Coll. I had written to Alastair Oliphant at the Coll Hotel and requested the use of his field behind the hotel, which we'd enjoyed (despite the weather) two years before. I had also ordered a few days' supplies from the two shops on Coll. After leaving home on a Friday evening in mid-August and making the now familiar change of stations in Glasgow, we reached Oban about noon on a cloudy but promising Saturday. We found the *Claymore* waiting at the quay, and set sail at 1pm.

By prearrangement, my sister Christine and a friend met us on board the *Claymore.* They were to sail with us to Coll, continue on to Tiree, and then return to Oban (see top photograph on page 97) that same evening. So, our lunch on the ship was, for me, a pleasant family occasion, as well as our first meal of the camp. After lunch, as we sailed up the Sound of Mull, the afternoon began to fulfil the promise of the morning. The sun came out, the calm water sparkled, and even over Mull – where cloud so often gathers – the sky became completely clear. Tobermory, which we had seen so often through sheets of rain in 1962, welcomed us with a bright and brilliant scene. There was fresh paint on the shops and houses, and many coloured sails of scores of yachts, preparing for a regatta. On the quayside was the Tiree Pipe Band, in full regalia. To our delight, the band boarded the *Claymore.* They were homeward bound after playing at the regatta, and for most of the voyage to Coll, we were entertained with tunes and dances on the deck. It was a most fitting welcome to Bonnie Scotland.

Coll was welcoming too, with brilliant afternoon sunshine, brightly coloured vehicles on the pier, and around them, small groups of excited people. I thought Coll must have been overrun with visitors, but that wasn't really so. By the time we had greeted Mr Oliphant and a few old friends, picked up our stores, and assembled our kit upon the land above the church, they all seemed to have disappeared, and Coll had returned to its usual state of perfect tranquillity. Looking out over the village to the blue sea and the panorama of islands, it was a day so clear that one could see the whole range of the Inner Hebrides, from the Cuillin Mountains on Skye to the Paps of Jura. I remember thinking, and saying, just how extraordinarily lucky we were.

The next day, Sunday, wasn't so pleasant – a little misty with a hint of rain. In the morning, we went to the Church of Scotland, which was no more than a stone's throw from our tents. I remember the congregation was considerable, and the minister was a woman. Afterwards, I spent half an hour in the hotel. The bar was dominated by a large and voluble gentleman who had been in church, and from the general conversation, it was apparent that he was a clergyman. Having done the rounds of everyone in the bar, he eventually came to me, sitting quietly in the corner. He wasted no time:

"What do you do?" he asked.

"I'm of your profession," I replied.

"Really?" he said. "What's your name?"

"Vanstone," I answered.

The effect of my answer caused a sensation. The large man banged his glass down on the bar. "Good heavens," he said, and then announced exuberantly to all present, "Here's the fellow who did me out of a job 20 years ago!"

This dramatic and, to me, surprising announcement, caused a great deal of interest. The man's name was McNaughton. He explained publicly that, when I wished to become curate of St Thomas' Church, Bolton, many years ago, he had also applied for the role, but he'd been the unlucky one. I felt rather ashamed of having been the cause of disappointment to such a jolly, friendly chap.

It was back to camp for lunch, which we served and ate in the rain, getting whatever shelter we could in the lee of the church. The afternoon continued wet and largely uneventful.

In the evening, I felt it right to attend the service at the Free Kirk. A number of the party came with me. We recalled our previous visit to that church two years before, when we had heard a memorable sermon from the Free Kirk minister, Mr McIver, just three days after he had miraculously survived a great storm that caught him in his open boat at sea. This time, the minister was different, and the sermon was very different too. It was beautifully constructed and eloquently delivered, but lasting almost a full hour, its subject was damnation. We all went to bed that evening rather chastened, cheered only by one good omen the day had brought. During the afternoon, Michael, David and I had taken a brief walk in the hills behind the camp, and we had found, for the first time ever on a camp, a clump of genuine white heather.

The next morning, our luck was in. It was another sparkling day, and the sky a heavenly blue with just the occasional white cloud drifting across it. On such a morning, Hebridean scenery is so clear and clean, and the Hebridean air so bracing. We spent the day walking a four-mile trek across the island to the *machir* and silver beach at Cliad on the other side of the island. During the walk, Stephen Francis was busy with our new camera. He took a series of bright, clear slides, which always bring back the lovely feel of that joyful morning. We padded along the quiet road, with our sandwiches packed in buckets, with nothing and no one to trouble us, and with almost the whole holiday still ahead. We lunched on the *machir* by the side of a ruined schoolhouse at Arnabost. Afterwards, we spent the afternoon on the beach and among the sandhills, lazing around, swimming and burying Stephen in the sand. On the walk back, I remember Stephen Andrews' determination to find some more white heather, although I'm afraid he wasn't in luck. Meanwhile, after tea, the day ended with a form of cricket on the same 'pitch' we had used two years before.

On the Tuesday, our plan was to go down to the great beach at Breachacha, at the south-west tip of the island, the site of a 15th century tower house and castle (see photograph on page 98). It was around seven miles away. Some of us had hired bikes from the hotel and were planning on cycling down, while Mr McNaughton had promised to take the rest of us by car. Unfortunately, he forgot. He showed his contrition later by sending us a most generous peace offering of shandy and crisps. After waiting over an hour with genuine Hebridean patience, we obtained the services of an ancient lorry to carry us to Breachacha. The six cyclists arrived before our lorry, and it was great to see them from the crest of the sand dunes, tearing up and down the firm sand of that great beach. There was no one else in sight, no one to endanger and no one to annoy. Here was freedom indeed.

Some of our party went swimming, but Michael and I cut away to one of the arms of the bay to search for the ancient burial ground of the MacLeans, as marked on the map. We found it. We also found some useful pieces of driftwood and some wild mushrooms. Best of all, we found the most colourful stretch of *machir* I've ever seen. In every square yard of the close-cropped turf there were hundreds of bright, tiny flowers of many kinds and every shade. I only wish we'd had the camera with us to take some close-ups of that lovely stretch of grass. It was a beautiful day at Breachacha.

Since our last visit to Coll, two years earlier, we found there had been a surprising number of changes in local society. Both ministers whom we had met in 1969 had left, along with the doctor. Sadly, the pier master had died, while Mrs Kennedy, who had given us those wonderful cakes, was in hospital on the mainland. The shop that had been owned by Mr and Mrs Sproat had been taken over by the hotel. But Neilly John was still around. Davey was also there (in the hotel pub) and Archie was still at the Free Kirk. With his usual kindness, Archie took David Whitehead fishing one afternoon, and they brought back mackerel for our evening meal. Mr MacDonald was still in the other shop, but rather gloomy about the future of Coll. On the other hand, Mr Oliphant was optimistic. There was a good deal of the island's enterprise originating from the hotel by now. For instance, Coll is the only one of the smaller islands where we've been able to buy decent postcards, which I believe are produced by the hotel. One of them sits in front of me now, as I write. I only wish we could have bought cards on Eigg, Canna, Colonsay or Barra to do equal justice to those islands too.

Our stay on Coll ended on the Wednesday morning. Apart from having some difficulty in locating Mr MacDonald to pay our bill, all went smoothly. And our regret at leaving was tempered by the hope of the unknown islands and unplanned days that lay ahead. The boat for Barra arrived on time, and the sea was calm. We lunched on board, near Tiree. As we sailed westwards, the sun came out, and I remember a delightful hour on deck, watching as the distant rocks of the Outer Hebrides came into view. Brent was a little queasy until we came under the lee of Barra, and the last half hour of the sail was perfect. Our entry into Castlebay, with its village and old castle, all soaked in sunshine, made for one of our happiest landfalls.

My only anxiety was over a site. Around Castlebay itself, there was little but bare rock. Our map suggested that we'd only be able to find a suitable spot on the western side of Barra, over four miles from the village. As we got off the boat, I remember saying to Michael, "Ideally, we need to find a man with a lorry who will be available in two hours' time when we've done our shopping, and who will then just drive us westwards until we find a spot." I had hardly spoken the words when I spotted a lorry on the quayside, its driver leaning on the vehicle. In one minute, everything was arranged. Two hours would suit the driver fine, and he'd drive us wherever we wanted to go.

The shops were busy, and for the first time, we heard Gaelic spoken extensively. We then piled aboard the lorry. While I sat in the cab talking to the driver and looking out for a site, I heard the not-so-gentle strains of 'On Ilkla Moor Baht 'at' being raised from the back of the lorry. I don't know why that particular song was chosen, but it no doubt accounted for John Stanczyk's curious question later that evening: "Are we at Ilkla Moor, Sir?"

In fact, we were at Borve, a crofting village on the west coast of Barra, camping on roughish *machir* between the village and the shore. On a mobile camp, it's always enjoyable when – after locating a site, pitching tents and enjoying a meal – one can then look around, at leisure, at the amenities and features of the site. This one was pleasant enough. Behind us, Beinn Mhartain rose to some 900 feet. At its foot, the village nestled in a lovely glen, while to the south, over the crest of the dunes, lay a long, silver beach with an adequate supply of driftwood for our fires. The only inconvenience was that the stream beside us was also the village sewer, but we overcame this challenge by asking for water at the schoolmistress's cottage.

We decided to spend two nights on Barra before moving on and crossing the Sound of Eriskay to South Uist (see bottom photograph on page 97). We had heard vague rumours of a ferry from the north of Barra, but we were several miles from the departure point. So, we devoted the following morning to planning. Michael walked into Castlebay with David and Stephen Francis to buy a new axe and draw some money from the post office. They also planned to engage the services of our lorry for the following morning. Meanwhile, I went to the phone box in Borve to make contact with the ferryman, Neil Campbell. It was a rather unsatisfactory line, and I hoped Mr Campbell could hear me better than I could hear him. I also recall that here, for the first time, I encountered the entirely trusting attitude of the Hebridean telephone authorities. When calling from the public phone box, you paid for the call after finishing it.

This done, I then called in the village shop. Not that we were short of anything, but on a mobile camp, the menu revolves around a limited range of items such as stewed steak, corned beef and tinned fruit. I was hoping, therefore, to pick up some unexpected delicacy. No such luck, though. The shop was well stocked, but only with three items: oatmeal, soap powder and pickles. There was no hope of anything else until the boat made its next call.

Michael and his party had a long walk to and from Castlebay, and it was after lunch when they returned to camp, almost dragging Stephen with them. He had an unpleasant pain in the stomach. This news brought back anxious thoughts of appendicitis and kept us around camp in the afternoon, except for a few energetic spirits, who either climbed Beinn Mhartain or played football on the *machir* nearby. Fortunately, by teatime, Stephen felt better, and so Michael and I walked up Beinn Mhartain. It was a lovely climb on a clear, sunny evening, and from the summit, it gave us a superb view of the whole of Barra, a stretch of South Uist, the peaks of Rhum to the east, and what I took to be the faint outline of either the Monach Islands or St Kilda to the west. For sheer extent, it was one of the finest views I've ever seen in the Hebrides. I remember how tiny, yet how homely, our little group of tents looked from almost 1,000 feet above. When we came down the hill, we ended the evening with a look at the simple Roman Catholic church that lay at its foot.

The next morning, the friendly driver pitched up with his lorry, according to plan. It was, in fact, a metal dump truck, not ideally suited to carrying passengers. Nonetheless, it transported us all safely north, up the coast of Barra and across the narrow neck of land at Eoligarry. It took us around the beach with its landing strip – surely the most primitive airport in Britain – and, finally, to a lonely headland at the extreme north of the island, with just a rough pier and a pile of gravel. There was no sign of the ferry boat, and as the lorry was about to drive away, it occurred to me that if the ferry did fail to show up, we'd be in for a rather uncomfortable time. Our food stocks were low and goodness knows how far we were from the nearest shop.

I voiced these fears to the driver, who replied, "Och...Neil generally comes."

We weren't altogether reassured by his reply.

After some time, there was still no sign of the ferry. I squatted behind a rock, sheltering from the fresh wind and brooding on our possible predicament.

Suddenly, a lively female voice rang in my ears with a clear, metallic New York accent: "Say...are you in charge of this wild crew?"

Looking round, I had to admit her description of my companions was perfectly reasonable. Andy Holt and Ian Ray – both tanned and with wind-swept, long hair – had the distinct look of a pair of young Vikings. If not exactly uncouth, these two were far from couth. Not that the woman and her husband were annoyed by our presence. They were delighted to find someone else at that world's end and seemed pleased that we too believed in both the ferry's existence and its possible arrival.

Soon, it came. The tiny boat approaching on that wide sea was piloted by Neil Campbell, a huge man who really did look like a Viking. Apparently, Mr Campbell knows more than anyone now alive about the wartime wreck of the *SS Politician* and of the days of *Whisky Galore!* on the nearby islands. He soon had us aboard, operating a kind of age distinction, which kept the boys in the stern and the two Americans and me in the bows.

I shall always remember that crossing. It was interesting enough in itself, with seals on the rocks, seabirds whirling, and the coastline and cottages of Eriskay. It was a fine, bright day with just enough swell to let us know we were at sea. But my companions in the bows were a delight too. They had left their car on South Uist, the previous day, and had come over to Barra on the ferry. They'd intended to catch the ferry back that evening, but had somehow missed it and had been stranded on Barra for the night. Some kindly souls had given them shelter in a cottage, but they'd had nothing to eat and were very hungry. I searched in the pouch of my anorak and found a few crumbling, unappetising biscuits. These were most gratefully accepted and enthusiastically eaten. I thought to myself, *Well, here I am, sailing one of the most romantic straits in the world, feeding biscuits to a couple of highly literary and sophisticated Jews from Manhattan.*

The Jewish couple were clearly well-read, witty and, to judge from the extended holiday they were having, rather wealthy too. It somehow came out in the conversation that I was a vicar.

"Ah gee," said the young woman, with delight. "I've always wanted to meet an English vicar; I've read so much about them in Jane Austen. Say, do you have land?"

I explained to the Americans that, no, I didn't have land, and our immediate objective was to locate a shop. We were almost out of supplies, and I'd heard shops on South Uist were few and far between. So, I had a more urgent objective, which was to find transport to get us to a shop, implying an even more urgent objective still – to find a telephone to hire transport to get us there. But here the Americans could help: their car was at the pier where we'd land, and they offered to run me to a phone and back again. It was as well that they did, since the nearest phone was at least 2.5 miles from Ludac, where we'd come ashore. We located the phone box, which for some strange reason, was in the middle of a field. I managed to contact a man in Lochboisdale who owned a bus. And as usual in the Hebrides, he was available immediately. He promised to pick us up at Ludac 30 minutes later.

While we were away at the phone, Tony had taken the lead in getting the Campingaz stoves going. He brewed coffee and managed to turn our last supplies of bread and cheese into decent sandwiches. He had included our American friends in the party, and I shall always remember how heartily they ate their very primitive meal, before driving off with many expressions of thanks. On our travels, we've had many fleeting encounters with strangers and none is pleasanter to recall than this.

As promised, our bus arrived, and the driver advised that any shopping for us would be better done in Creagorry, Benbecula. So, we crossed the whole of South Uist – from south to north – in one stage. From the road, however, you don't see the glories of South Uist, including a 20-mile stretch of silver sand along its western shore, its trout-filled lochs and the island's multitude of rare wild flowers. You just experience an endless line of sand dunes on one side and a rough, flat moor of heather on the other. During the hour-long drive, however, we did spot the fine, new Roman Catholic church at Bornish, as well as Huw Lorimer's great statue *Our Lady of the Isles*, which we stopped to photograph. We were all happy, I think, that we weren't going to camp on South Uist.

But we were quite disappointed when the bus left us at Creagorry: it was probably the least favourite of all our camp sites. Admittedly, there were two shops where we could replenish our supplies, and just outside the village, we found a patch of flat grass between road and shore that was just big enough for our tents. Otherwise, there was little to recommend Creagorry, with its surrounding land so flat, the road so straight, and the village dominated by noise and smell of a most un-Hebridean pub.

New construction work was being carried out there in connection with the army's rocket range on South Uist. And that work had brought an influx of workers and cash to Creagorry, but most of the money seemed to go on whisky. At lunchtime, when we arrived, and in the evening too, the pub was spilling drunks and noise around the village.

It was a windy day, and I remember we had a job to pitch our tents. It was late afternoon before we had cooked and eaten a welcome meal. I lost no time in the evening in securing a minibus from Lochmaddy to North Uist for the following morning. That night, we watched cockle gatherers at work as the tide went out over the great strand between Benbecula and South Uist. We followed suit, and so for those who fancied them, there were boiled cockles for supper.

We were away the following morning, a Saturday, travelling again over the flatness of Benbecula and across the causeway to North Uist (see top photograph on page 99). But as we turned eastwards towards Lochmaddy, the countryside became more hilly and more interesting. We arrived about 11.30am, and Lochmaddy seemed a cosy spot for the weekend. There were a couple of shops, a decent pub and a post office, where our first mail was waiting for us. We secured a site on some land behind the pub and pitched camp on the edge of the rocks that rose in a miniature cliff, some 20 feet out of the water. Of all our sites, this one was the closest to the sea. From our 'kitchen' on a ledge on the little cliff, we looked directly down into 10 feet of crystal-clear water.

There was climbing, swimming and diving there, with gentle rambling around a jigsaw of water and land to the west of Lochmaddy. It was a curious mix of landscape and seascape, which was notable for an enormous amount of seaweed on the edge of the tidal lochs, and with deep holes and erosions in the peat on land. From our site, the view was splendid. To our left, Lochmaddy widened to the open sea, while in front stood the three highest peaks of North Uist on the far side of the water. Although, so near to the village, it was ever so lovely and quiet. We were completely undisturbed there, camping on the water's edge.

Sunday in Lochmaddy was a Sabbath indeed. It was a grey day, and when I walked through the village about 11.30am, the emptiness and silence were almost oppressive. There wasn't a soul in the streets, not a door was open, and no cars passed by. Some 20 minutes later, as I came back through the village, doors began to open, and sombre, black-clad figures, Bibles in their hands, moved silently and thoughtfully to the

Gaelic service at the kirk. I knew that we were in country where the duties of religion are taken with deep seriousness. There had been evidence enough in the two shelves of books on sale at one of the two shops: every book had a religious theme. I hadn't bargained, however, for such intensity and quiet of the Sabbath. As I came nearer the camp, I met one man clearly not bound for the kirk. The man, a Londoner, had just come ashore – by rubber dinghy – from his yacht moored in the bay. His small party was cruising round the Hebrides, he said, and he'd come ashore in search of a drink. I'd have laughed, but it seemed rather frivolous to do so.

Instead, I said gravely, "You'll not get a drink here on a Sunday."

"Rubbish," he replied. "Even if they won't serve the locals, they'll serve travellers."

"Well, you can ask," I said. "I'm not going to."

I watched him walk into the hotel where the manager was startled at his request, and the Londoner the same at the refusal.

I took him back to camp on the chance of coffee. Tony, I remember, was cooking dinner, and the Londoner was just as amazed at the possibility of cooking dinner on driftwood as he had been at the impossibility buying beer on Sunday. It must have been his first visit north of Oxford and certainly his first to the Hebrides.

In the evening, when the service was to be conducted in English, we went to the kirk. Once again, it was a well-attended and well-conducted service, with a good sermon.

A gentleman behind us kept agreeing with the sentiment of the minister and every so often, came out with a loud and distinct, "Hear hear!"

The following morning, it was still grey, but life had returned to the village. We had to do some more shopping. In one of the shops, I was buying shortbread biscuits when a lady came in and commented on my purchase.

"Those look nice," she pointed out to me.

"They are nice," I replied. "We've had some before. Let's open a packet and have one now."

My companions had a biscuit, and we offered one to the lady.

"Very nice…I shall buy some," she said.

We left the shop, and a few minutes later, I was talking to the minister in the street. The same lady came past in a car and waved. Whether she was waving to me or the minister, I didn't know, but the minister took it she was waving to me.

"Och!" he said. "Then, you'll know Lady Dunrossil?"

"Well," I explained, "I don't exactly know her, but I've just given her a biscuit."

"Aye," he said. "Maybe you'd know her husband was Speaker of the House of Commons during the war."

We were to leave Lochmaddy on the Monday night on the car ferry to Skye. We thought it would be good to see a little more of North Uist before leaving, so in the late afternoon, we hired a sort of van with windows for a drive around the island. We saw a few deer on the moor and an area on the western shore where bulb growing was being developed, but it wasn't a particularly interesting drive. I've since read in one of the guidebooks that this particular road misses the interesting parts of North Uist, which are a couple of miles off the beaten track. We were a little unlucky.

We were unlucky too with the boat that night. It was due at 10pm, but it didn't arrive until three hours later. We killed time in the waiting room on the quay by talking to a man from Berneray, the largest and only populated island in the Sound of Harris. He was off for a week's holiday in Glasgow. We chatted about lobster fishing and life on Berneray, as well as our friend's experiences as a seaman. It turned out that, in 1962, he had been part of the crew of a luxury yacht – which we had named 'the floating gin palace' – that had been moored in Tobermory Bay while we camped at Aros on Mull. During that weekend, the weather had been so appalling that it had stuck in our friend's mind. He remembered being sorry for the privations of us in our tents, as we remembered being envious of the apparent comfort onboard that yacht.

We had intended to sleep on the deck of the *SS Hebrides* that night, but the deck was hard, cold and cheerless. Better counsel prevailed. A few cabins were still available, and we packed in – four to a cabin, with juniors on bunks and seniors on the floor – and we all got a decent night's sleep.

We woke at Uig in Skye on a bright morning that got better and better as the minutes and hours went by. We were aiming for Portree and found a public bus that would take us there, although there was some difficulty in packing all our kit in the boot. I enjoyed that ride – our first on the Isle of Skye (see bottom photograph on page 99) – and we were seeing the island at its best. By the time we reached Portree, the sky was cloudless, and the sun was hot. By contrast to the tiny villages we normally experienced in the Hebrides, Portree was a metropolis. We found a café for mid-morning snacks, and then there was the matter of finding a site. Tents were visible on a shoreline, about a mile to the east. At Portree's Tourist Information Office, nobody knew who owned the land, but we decided that if others could camp there, so could we. I arranged transport to arrive in 30 minutes, and we waited, sitting and lying sleepily on the steps of the memorial.

And then I had a delightful surprise. Two of my oldest friends, Jack and Winnie Crook, whom we had also met on Arran in 1967, suddenly appeared from nowhere. It was lovely to see them. We had time for a quick drink and a hilarious chat in the nearest pub before our transport arrived. Our meeting was, once again, one of those totally unexpected moments of delight that our camps have so often brought.

Furthermore, our camp site was lovely too. Our tents were within a stone's throw of the sea, and we faced south, across the loch, which offered a full, magnificent view of the Cuillin Mountains in all their grandeur. Behind us, a cliff rose fairly steeply. I didn't climb it myself, but the energetic spirits who did reported impressive views to the north. Someone spotted a white deer. There was swimming in the afternoon, and a couple of boats were hired. I watched on from the site, delighting in the deep-blue water, the brown and purple of the hills beyond, and the huge, cloudless sky.

Later, I had the pleasure of meeting even more friends. The Revd and Mrs David Ashworth had heard from the Crooks of our presence and came out to see us. They'd been chatting earlier to people who knew Skye well and who'd said they'd never seen it on such a lovely day.

It was, indeed, a great day, and the next morning brought the promise of another just as good. We decided to stay where we were for just one more night, and then make tracks. A few of us walked down into the village for coffee and were on the way to the shops when we heard running feet behind us. It was Andy, hotfooting it from the camp. The owner of the land had suddenly appeared, and not mincing his words, had ordered all tents to be removed within an hour. There was nothing we could do and little point in arguing. And in any case, when I got back to the site, the owner had vanished. So, we packed up, got the kit down to the village and decided to move on to Armadale for the night.

There was an hour or two before the bus left, and just enough time for a picnic lunch and a quick drink in a pub on the quay. Highland Games were taking place in Portree the following day, and the town was full of pipers. In the pub, I had the pleasure of talking to two fine old chaps who were to be judges for the piping competition. Their talk was of pipers they'd known over the years, of deer forests and notable stalkers, and of winters in the Cairngorms and fishing in Argyll. They might have come straight from the pages of a John Buchan novel. And although much of their talk was of shooting, they were in no way callous of any suffering they caused. They deplored hunters who fired at too distant a range, causing injury instead of instant death. One spoke with regret of the only time in his life when he'd shot a seal. It was to be the first and last time he ever did that, he said with sorry eyes. It was an interesting conversation, showing a type of man I've rarely, if ever, met before.

The bus was a weary old banger, much given to grinding gears and stalling on hills, but the scenery of our ride to Armadale was superb. Still, there wasn't a cloud in the sky. It was a pleasant, sleepy drive, but as we came towards our destination, I began to be a little anxious about finding a site. There was no obvious site, nor a shop nearby. I envisaged a great deal of walking around and searching on that hot afternoon.

Meanwhile, the bus had deposited us at the pier, where a ferry to Mallaig was about to leave. I suddenly had an idea and proposed it to the company. We had said we'd be home, probably by Friday. Should we change our plan, go over to Mallaig right now and have a meal in the familiar café? We could spend the night at the site just outside the village and return home on Thursday?

I was tired enough to be pleased when the proposal was accepted. Within two minutes, we were on the ferry. It was a brief but beautiful sail, and I'm glad to have some photographs of the crossing in my book of treasures. After a meal in the café in Mallaig, we pitched three tents at the spot we'd discovered the previous year, on the cliff beside a children's playground, some 600 yards from the little port.

As the sun set that night over the southern tip of Skye, we watched from the cliffs for a long time. It was a most beautiful sunset, and the evening matched our mood of contentment at reaching the mainland again, after a successful but quite difficult journey. Though we were still more than 300 miles away, we almost felt as if we had reached home.

There were still one or two more incidents. During the night, Ian Ray was wakened and saw a couple of figures prowling round the tents. His shout wakened me.

I shouted – cunningly, I thought – *"Keep the dog back!"* but it was probably Ian's shout rather than fear of a non-existent dog that made the intruders run off.

Most of our kit was stacked outside the tents, so for safety's sake, I slept beside the kit for an hour or two, until the heavy dew of early morning made me seek the shelter of a tent.

On the journey home, we spent a long time queuing in Glasgow Central Station and chatting with a Canadian couple from Alberta. Our train had been delayed for a couple of hours on its journey from the south, but the railway staff did a quick turnaround in Glasgow, and we picked up more time on the run home to Manchester. We weren't so late on arrival there, and when we finally reached home, how can I ever forget my utter surprise and delight on finding that, in my absence, my house had been redecorated secretly and kindly by our curate (Mr Samuels) and the Men's Guild.

It had been a good journey. We had taken in a broad sweep of the Hebrides and had formed a firmer impression of the differences between the Hebrides and of the uniqueness of each island. It was my conclusion that the most attractive islands were the smaller ones, where one is always conscious of the nearness of the sea and where islanders live as one community, almost as one family. It was this conclusion that directed our attention to two of the smallest islands, Eigg and Canna, as possible sites for the forthcoming year. But before telling that story, I must record the full list of those who travelled with me on the tour of 1971, namely Michael Daman, David Francis, Stephen Francis, Andy Holt, Tony Layton, Ian Ray, Ian Aitchison, Stephen Andrews, David Whitehead, Brent Andrews, Gerald Hinchcliffe and John Stanczyk.

# Chapter 8

We had visited the Isle of Eigg before, and spent a couple of good days there, at the end of the touring camp in 1970. We had arrived then without any prearrangement or permission. But in 1972, since we hoped to be a rather larger party and to stay a little longer, I thought it best to make some prior arrangements. First, I contacted the Roman Catholic priest, Father Barrett-Leonard, whom we had met on the island during our first visit. I discovered from him that ownership lay with the Anglyn Trust, a somewhat mysterious body whose *raison d'être* we never fully understood. However, I contacted the director of that trust, and we were given permission to stay for five or six days near our previous site on the Bay of Laig.

As to the Isle of Canna, I already knew a good deal from the guidebooks about its laird, Dr Lorne Campbell. When I wrote to him, asking if we might come, I received a charming reply, not only giving ready permission but also mentioning certain points about Canna of which we needed to be aware – in particular, its lack of a shop. We were already aware of this, and the planning of this camp involved careful and systematic shopping in Rochdale beforehand, so we had everything that might be difficult to obtain on Eigg, and impossible on Canna. These were packed into two large and heavy tea chests, which I thought might cause some difficulty when crossing over from Glasgow Central Station to Glasgow Queen Street.

The difficulty, however, didn't arise, for when we sorted out all the complexities of boat and train times, we found there would be no change of stations: we would enter Glasgow at Queen Street after travelling through York and Edinburgh. Even so, could we be in Mallaig in time to catch the boat for Eigg on the Monday? The most straightforward way of getting to York involved hiring a rather expensive, special bus. At least that meant we could leave for camp straight after Sunday evening service – something I'd never done before but had always wanted to do.

I shall long remember that evening. We had a good evensong, followed by a quick cup of coffee. We gave our good wishes to parents and friends before piling on to the bus and setting off on the motorway through Leeds, and then on to York.

The party numbered 16, including Peter Holme, Frank Hammond and Stephen Ashworth, whom it was good to have with us after a break of a year or two. The rest included Michael Daman, Andy Holt, Ian Aitchison, Stephen Andrews, Stephen Francis, Brent Andrews, David Whitehead, David Holt, Philip Taylor, Shaun Andrews, Peter Scott, Jerry Whitsey and me. Our four youngest members were camping for the first time. I remember thinking, as we set off, that most youngsters have their first taste of camp somewhere rather less remote and romantic than Hebridean islands such as Eigg and Canna.

The overnight journey to the north was uneventful, except for our uncertainty – evidently shared by railway officials – as to whether we should change in Edinburgh. In fact, we did change at Edinburgh, but after drinking a terrible cup of tea from a platform trolley at about 4am, we then got back on the same train, though from a different platform. Daylight came as we left Glasgow. A heavy drizzle that morning made the track towards the summit of Rannoch Moor very slippery. It caused the train to grind along and slip alarmingly as it strained along the track, assisted at one point by a man walking alongside the railway line and throwing sand under the wheels. We lost half an hour from the delay and with it what chance we had of having lunch in Mallaig. All our time went in carting our kit to the pier and in ordering bread and other perishables to be shipped out to us at Canna on the following Monday.

When I ventured to pay for this order, a matter of £8, the shop manager said, "Will ye no' be coming back this way?"

"Yes," I answered, "but in about a fortnight."

"Och," he said. "Ye could pay for it then."

This little incident sticks in my mind as being characteristic of the complete trust with which we were treated for the next two weeks.

When the *Loch Arkaig* sailed for Eigg at 1pm, the ship seemed crowded. We became aware of another party of campers also bound for Eigg. A group with similar numbers to our own, we gathered they were from King Edward VI School, Birmingham. Their clothing and equipment were superb, as well they might be, since they were described on the labels as "The Expedition to the Isle of Eigg". Of this party, more anon. For the present, our main concern was with the weather, rather than our fellow passengers.

After the drizzle of the morning, the sky was still grey as we left Mallaig, but there was a familiar brightness to the west, which gave hope of better things to come. The hope didn't disappoint since, as we drew away from the mainland, clouds broke and patches of blue appeared. By the time we were passing the eastern cliffs of Eigg, the sun was giving us a splendid welcome.

As we were watching for the ferry coming out from Eigg, I became aware of a young man – evidently, a foreigner – trying in vain to put some point to a member of crew. He sounded like a Frenchman, so I offered in my best schoolboy French my services as interpreter. This was a mistake, for the young man then deluged me in French, and the seaman made a crafty getaway. The general drift of the Frenchman's query was "Is this Kyle of Lochalsh?"

It was my painful duty to inform him, with some assistance in vocabulary from my companions, that this was certainly not the Kyle of Lochalsh, and that he'd have to return to Mallaig and start again. But before reaching Mallaig at 9pm, he'd have to circumnavigate Eigg, Rhum and Canna.

The Frenchman was disconcerted: "Where am I to sleep tonight?"

We suggested the railway station at Mallaig.

This did seem to please him. *"Mais...y a t'il, peut-être, un gare sur Rhum?"*[iii] he asked.

The notion of a railway station on Rhum was too ridiculous to contemplate. We had to leave him, uncomforted, but at least we were able to explain to the purser that he had accidentally got on the wrong boat, and to arrange for his fare to be returned.

It took the small ferry two trips to get us all ashore. I came on the second. When I came ashore, I noticed that, while members of the 'Expedition' were restless and impatient to get to their campsite, our own party had settled down comfortably, and were simply ready to hang around and wait. They'd got used to Hebridean ways and had acquired the islanders' art of patience. We needed a great deal of patience that afternoon before we got everybody and everything over to the Bay of Laig. Both a van and a tractor were involved in transporting us across the island. Each had to make the trip across the island twice, which meant that each had to pass the shop four times. Since it's considered a sin, if not a crime, to pass the shop on Eigg without stopping for a chat and a can of beer, it was some considerable time before the last of our party – namely Peter, Stephen and Frank – arrived at the Bay of Laig with the last of our kit.

We pitched our tents 200 yards south of the spot where we'd had them in 1970, on the rough *machir* behind the crest of the low dunes. There was a good stream just to the south of us, and we left the other stream and the north end of the bay to the Expedition boys, whose fine tents soon appeared above the rocks that bounded that edge of the bay. There was time, while waiting for the last of the kit, to take in and photograph that simply glorious site, which was no less impressive for being already familiar. There again stood the great amphitheatre of cliffs behind us, while the peaks of Rhum rose majestically in front, across the blue water. After so many camps, in so many places, I still think that the site on the Bay of Laig is the finest we've ever had. And

---

iii "But... is there, perhaps, a railway station on Rhum?"

it's no surprise that on the front cover of the book *The Hebrides* (by WH Murray)[11] is the same view on the Bay of Laig that greeted us every morning as we emerged out of our tents.

We were on Eigg from Monday evening until Saturday. Let's get over the unpleasant bits first. We faced on the Wednesday continuous rain, driving in from the south-west. It was that kind of penetrating drizzle that blocks one's view and locates any weak spot in clothing or tents. The tents stood up to the rain very well, as did the juniors, who spent nearly all day in their tents without fuss or disorder. The rest of us kept the fire going and cooked, although we did get wetter and wetter as the day went on. By 5.30pm, I decided I'd had enough. So, we abandoned the fire and made the last drink of the day on the Campingaz stove in Michael's tent. It felt good to be inside, and we couldn't help feeling a little complacent on hearing that the Expedition had abandoned its site that day and had taken refuge in the island's school.

We had similar conditions on the Saturday when leaving Eigg, but apart from those two days, the weather stayed good. So, what did we do? There was swimming, of course, and lots of cricket on that splendid beach. Play was held up one morning by the appearance of an otter, which trotted calmly along the beach before going into the sea for a swim. There was also an evening walk to the singing sands on the north-west of the island. We walked along the shore, once again, among those fantastically eroded rocks, which seemed even more impressive than on our last visit. We returned to camp along the cliff top. In the course of the walk, I remember winning – or, at any rate, I deserved to win – a large bet, by standing under a waterfall, fully clothed.

On another glorious afternoon, we headed along the shore – this time, heading south in search of driftwood. We were in luck and found plenty that day. Brent also found a fine fish basket in the surf. It proved useful for the rest of the camp and, eventually, made its way home with us. In the later stages of the walk, we located spectacular cliff scenery, which provided some of the best of our colour slides.

We spent the best part of one day climbing the Sgùrr of Eigg, the highest hill on the island, standing at a height of just under 1,300 feet.

It was a decent walk of about 11 miles, most of it rough going over bog and heather. I had discussed the walk previously with Roddy, one of two local men who appear to do all the jobs on the island – from working the ferry to mending the roads. I discovered that Roddy had never walked up An Sgùrr in his life. What's more, he regarded it as a formidable enterprise that no one should undertake for pleasure. However, it did give us some fine views and a wonderful sense of space and freedom when we finally reached the summit. Soon enough, however, passing clouds brought a scud or two of rain. While crouching for shelter behind some rocks, we realised that the Sgùrr of Eigg could be a bleak and cruel place in the wrong kind of weather.

I recall with pleasure a morning when Michael and I walked to the shop to phone Dr Campbell on Canna and confirm that we would be arriving on Saturday. The shop, which was also a pub and post office, was a telephone exchange as well, but to make the call one had to go into the kiosk across the road. I did so, and a hilarious 10 minutes followed. The complexities of using that phone were considerable. Every time I wanted the Eigg Exchange, Michael had to run across to the shop and persuade an assistant to leave her customers and attend to the switchboard. When, eventually, I got through to the post-office-cum-telephone-exchange on Canna, further confusion ensued, since the postmistress had a man's voice. What I took to be a man saying he'd get the post mistress was, in fact, the postmistress herself. When I gave my name, the good lady became quite excited because she thought I was a German by the name of Behr Kopf for whom a letter was waiting on Canna. Further confusion reigned. Eventually, I established that I wished to speak to Dr Campbell.

"That will be difficult," the lady said, "because Dr Campbell has two houses, and the one where the telephone is isn't the one where he lives."

This seemed like a curious arrangement, but the difficulty was solved by the postmistress's promise that she'd go to the house where Dr Campbell lived and personally deliver my message.

On our last evening at the Bay of Laig, we were challenged by the Expedition to a football match on the beach. The teams were around 16-a-side, but the pitch was easily large enough to have taken teams of 160 players. Our boys gained a satisfactory victory of 3–1, and I recall that Philip Taylor was one of our stars. He stood up most manfully to the assaults of the three rugger-playing masters who provided most of the opposition's attack. With Philip's keen defence, and excellent attacking play by our forwards, I had a peaceful time in goal. In fact, I spent most of the second half watching an ominous build-up of cloud from the south-west. I concluded we were in for some dirty weather.

We were. We were due to leave for Canna about 2pm on the *Western Isles*, a converted fishing smack, which replaces the *Loch Arkaig* on the Canna run on Saturdays. As the rain and wind increased that morning, I began to wonder whether the *Western Isles* would be able to sail. Michael went on a wet walk to the shop to sound local opinion, and everyone seemed to agree: yes, the ferry would be going. So, we packed up in some discomfort, got the kit to the quay on the tractor and ate our lunch in the shelter of a primitive bothy on the quayside. By the time the *Western Isles* arrived, the wind and rain were a fearsome double act, and I remember how we all huddled together on the ferry, under a tiny deck up in the bows. Mr Smith of the Anglyn Trust was on the quay to wave us off, and so was the doctor, who entrusted me with a couple of packages for Dr Campbell. Otherwise, the quay was deserted – a most unusual state of affairs when a boat comes in, anywhere in the Hebrides.

The ferry manoeuvred alongside the *Western Isles*. In the heavy swell, it wasn't easy to get aboard, and we were chivvied to, "Make haste," by a woman in oil skins on deck. Since a party of Guides were about to disembark, I took her for their captain. Her commanding manner filled me with respect. Respect soon turned to awe when, dissatisfied with our progress, she leaned over the gunwale, took hold of the rope that tied the tea chest Frank and Stephen were struggling with, and with one hand, yanked it aboard. She repeated the performance with the other chest. When we reached Canna, she picked up half a hundredweight of potatoes from the deck, threw it ashore and knocked Frank over. It turned out that the woman wasn't a Guide captain at all, but a member of the crew of the *Western Isles*. In fact, she constituted one half of the crew, and despite her trim figure, she must have been the strongest woman I've ever seen.

Beneath the rain-swept deck of the *Western Isles* was a small hold that served as the crew's quarters, the galley and a refuge for passengers. Until we reached Rhum, where a party of naturalists disembarked, the hold was too crowded to sort out who was who. But then, we realised there were only six other passengers on board bound for Canna. There were two ornithologists who became our good friends, and more of them anon. There were also two lighthouse keepers, who were planning to go to Heiskir but were blocked because of the weather. And finally, there was a Roman Catholic priest who visits Canna every month to say Mass, accompanied by a Roman Catholic bishop who was to conduct a confirmation on the island the following day. These last two were braving the conditions on deck, while the rest of us huddled in the hold, sprawled on primitive bunks, with some asleep and the others being sick. Occasionally, we'd come up on deck for a breath of fresh air or an attempt to steady our queasiness by fixing eyes on the horizon. However, on coming up, we simply faced sheets of rain, swirling mist and showers of spray as the *Western Isles* rolled until the deck seemed almost vertical. I was surprised we weren't all sick, but in fact, only a few succumbed to the rolling sea. However, I know we were all grateful when, after about 1.5 hours, we came under the lee of Sanday, before eventually entering the calm water of Canna's deep harbour.

I had looked forward to arriving at an island that I had heard so much about, but the conditions we faced didn't lend themselves to gazing round with any appreciation. It was still raining very hard in a strong, cold wind, and I didn't like the prospect of pitching tents that night. I didn't think Canna would possess a village hall, but if only there were a barn or bothy, or any primitive shelter we could borrow? I resolved to ask Dr Campbell as soon as he had finished welcoming the bishop onto the rain-swept quay.

I handed over the packages from the doctor on Eigg and enquired about a barn.

Dr Campbell shook his head: there was no barn at all. Then, he added, and how welcome were his words, "Of course, you could use the bothy. I don't know whether it will be big enough, but there's an upstairs room. It'll be in rather a mess, but there's water laid on, and I think you'll find some Calor Gas."

I needed to hear no more. Under such conditions, the bothy sounded like heaven, especially when the good doctor pointed out where it was – only 200 yards away from the quay. It was a low, white building, overhung by trees and looking out over the harbour.

Ten minutes later, we were in the bothy. It was, in fact, an old cottage at the end of a little row of former farm buildings. As bothies go, it was just fine. Upstairs was a bare but quite large room, which – when swept out – was assigned to the juniors. Downstairs, there was a sink, a stove, a table, a couple of chairs and, strangely, two beds. It wasn't exactly spacious, but it was cosy. It wasn't long before we were all sitting round, each with a big plate of corned beef hash, feeling a great deal better than a few hours before.

We discussed our plans for Sunday. The confirmation would be a big day in the island's life, so even if the weather was fine, we must not be bothering people for a tractor to get our kit to the camp site. It would be better, we decided, if we stayed in the bothy until Monday. The priest had apologised for not inviting all of us to the confirmation, as there would simply not be enough room in the tiny church. So, it seemed fitting that our two Roman Catholic members – Philip and Peter – should represent us at the confirmation, and that we should hold our own service in the bothy.

We then had to work out how 10 of us could find the space to sleep within the four walls of that tiny room downstairs. Jerry and Stephen Francis volunteered to join the juniors upstairs, while the two beds were allocated, by some now-forgotten principle, to Stephen Ashworth and Michael Daman. The rest of us achieved what space we could among and under the chairs, tables, rucksacks and other impedimenta with which we were so liberally furnished. But we slept, or at least I did, like dormice.

We woke to a glorious morning. Michael and I were up first, and we took a little stroll eastwards along the shore. We were intrigued by a large mass of rock jutting out into the sea at the top of which there seemed to be some kind of walled enclosure. A narrow sheep track led up to the top, and there was a sharp drop on the seaward side of the track.

At the top, I said to Michael, "I don't think we'd better let the juniors come here alone, as they could have a nasty fall, if they slipped."

Michael added, "Yes, and the stonework of the enclosure doesn't look too safe either."

We came down, and I put the rock out of bounds to our younger end. Only later did we come to know where we had been and what a fearsome and perilous reputation belongs to that little path we had climbed. For the enclosure on top of the rock was, in fact, the tower, famous in song and story where a laird of Canna of long ago is supposed to have confined his unfaithful wife. The ascent to the tower was fearsomely and dramatically described by Thomas Pennant, an 18th-century Hebrides traveller. He wrote of "a little tower at a vast height above us, accessible by a narrow and horrible path".[12]

Meanwhile, Sir Walter Scott – in his narrative poem, *The Lord of the Isles* – refers to the following:

> *Canna's tower that, steep and gray,*
> *Like falcon's nest o'erhangs the bay.*
> *Seek not the giddy crag to climb.*
> *To view the turret scarred by time.*
> *It is a task of doubt and fear.*
> *To aught but goat or mountain-deer.*[13]

We didn't think it all that bad, and I remember Dr Campbell's doubts as to whether Pennant had ever actually visited Canna. One suspects he wrote of that 'tower' from hearsay and that Scott himself had most likely copied what he'd read in Pennant, adding a few romantic imaginative touches. To us, the tower didn't seem anything like a falcon's nest.

We held our communion service, simply but carefully, that Sunday morning in the bothy. A little afterwards, Philip and Peter went off to the confirmation service in the tiny church. Once disused, and now recently restored, the wee chapel stands some 200 yards down the rough track that is, in fact, Canna's main road. In the meantime, we began to cook lunch on the shore in front of the bothy, and for some reason, we had all kinds of trouble. The fire wouldn't go properly, the pots wouldn't boil, and when we eventually opened the tins of roast beef that we'd saved especially for Sunday, we found them rather miserable and inadequate. Philip and Peter, I remember, were late for lunch because the confirmation had been followed by a party in the farmhouse beside the church. Refreshments apparently included lobster, cream cakes and Coca Cola.

Brent was a little off colour that afternoon, and Frank stayed with him in the bothy. The rest of us had a long walk to the adjoining island of Sanday, across the little causeway where a solitary electric lamp burns day and night at the shrine. People still leave coins there as they pass between the two islands, going past the croft of Mary Flora Steele, along with her two cows, and past several empty, tumbling crofts. We made first for the Roman Catholic church, an imposing building seen from the harbour, but now no longer used, since the tiny chapel on Canna suffices for the present population. We made for the rocky shore, where there was diving and swimming, and the camera was much in use on such a glorious afternoon. The coasts of Canna and Sanday, with Rhum in the background, looked so very beautiful across the blue water. It was a lovely treat to sit and look on. Apart from a couple of men who had come across from Canna in a boat, we had the whole landscape to ourselves. On the way home, I remember, we met

Mary Flora Steele talking to her two cows, and on a little hillside, we found clover, scabious and selfheal, which made a rich pattern of pink and blue among the grass.

It had been a good walk, and there was some talk of another walk after tea. But in fact, we started chatting in the bothy, and Frank related a long conversation with a lobster fisherman he'd had during that afternoon. One thing led to another, and the whole party gathered around in the fading light. The evening passed away with ghost stories and other tall tales.

On Monday morning, it was arranged that the tractor would come about 10am to take our kit along to the campsite. But before it arrived, a few of us inspected the church that stood between the bothy and the quay. Sailing into the harbour, one notices two churches. The one on the left is the Roman Catholic church on Sanday, which we'd visited the previous day and found to be no longer in use. The other, on the right, is a Church of Scotland, and when we tried the door, although open, we found that church also no longer used. Its roof and walls were intact, but parts of the floor had perished, while dust lay thick on the pews. It intrigued us to see the alms' dish in front of the pulpit with around £5 worth of dust-covered notes. We gathered later that the church is still used occasionally by visitors arriving by yacht, and that any money given is simply left there until Mrs Campbell collects it and sends it off to a charity. Yet another example of Hebridean trust! Apparently, this church was built only a couple of generations ago by a laird who was himself a Protestant. It can never have been well attended, for Canna has always been a predominantly Catholic island. Pennant says that, in his time, when the population was 220, all except four families were Roman Catholic.[14] At present, the population is 22, and all are Roman Catholic.

It's interesting to note that Pennant said both the Protestant minister and the 'popish priest' lived on Eigg, but they only visited Canna when the weather permitted.[15] Irrespective of whoever arrived on the little island – Protestant or Catholic priest – all the islanders attended the service. It's difficult to imagine this happening anywhere in Britain in the 18th century, except in the Hebrides.

When the tractor and trailer arrived, we all climbed onboard with our kit and bumped along the 'main road'. It opened out to a delightful, green valley to the south, about a mile from the bothy. There was bracken all around, but a sufficient area of short, smooth grass and a stream of good, clear water. We were some 200 yards from the shore and high enough to have a splendid view across Sanday to the peaks of Rhum. Canna is, by reputation, the greenest of all the Hebridean islands, and when our tents were up, and the fire was going, I felt once more how very fortunate we were with our site.

There were already two small tents on the site, belonging to the two ornithologists whom we had met onboard the *Western Isle*. They were sleeping after a night on the cliffs, ringing shearwaters. I'm sure they weren't exactly delighted when wakened by our noise, but they emerged with their customary cheerfulness, and became our good friends, with their presence only adding to our pleasure. Their names were Andrew and Robert, and they were from the University of Aberdeen. They impressed us with the way they combined their scientific attitude to ornithology with a most gentle way with the birds themselves. They didn't spare themselves in the pursuit of knowledge, going out for hours on the wild nights onto those dangerous cliffs, to find and ring shearwaters. They seemed to sleep little and didn't appear to eat much either. We pressed them into sharing our meals when they were around. One night, they brought a shearwater back to camp for us to see and photograph. I remember with what care they released the bird afterwards and watched to make sure it got safely out to sea. Not for anything would they hurt one of their beloved birds.

To Andrew and Robert, we owe a memorable walk. They told us of a cliff towards the western end of Canna where eagles can sometimes be seen. At the foot of the cliff are the ruins of an ancient nunnery. They told us that the cliff path was difficult and offered to be our guides. So, we set off one morning with sandwiches, a couple of Campingaz stoves and a whole day in front of us in new territory. We walked westwards along a track running between the shore and the cliffs, while Andrew and Robert identified the birds for us, including several chiffchaffs. I found pink yarrow and pink selfheal, and we stood by the side of the track while Hector, a local shepherd, came the other way with hundreds of sheep. It was excellent to watch Hector's sheepdogs working the flock so intelligently and obediently.

After a couple of miles, the track at the foot of the cliffs ended. For the next mile, we walked a little inland, up a broad hillside, which was home to some fine Highland cattle. The coast curved round to meet our path, and here, at the cliff top, our guides paused. Without them, we should never have found the little path that led down. Even if we had located it, I doubt if we'd have attempted it. It was a narrow sheep track snaking down cliffs that, although grassy, were exceedingly steep. I said some firm words about keeping in single file, concentrating on what we were doing and not chatting. But I doubt if my words were necessary. Everyone moved down carefully and quietly, without hurry and quite confidently. It was the same story when we came back again. Nevertheless, both at the bottom and, later, at the top, I breathed a deep sigh of relief.

Once safely at the bottom of the cliffs, we watched while Andrew and Robert found the nests of shags deep among the boulders and, with strong and sure hands, drew out the young birds for ringing. They showed us a peregrine falcon soaring above us, but eagles weren't to be seen on that day.

After a picnic lunch, Andrew and Robert left us to go further along the cliffs, while we explored the old nunnery. We detected a rough outer wall, still standing several feet high and enclosing a circle some 25 yards across. Inside it were several small circles of four or five yards in diameter. There was a spring with a certain amount of stonework around it, and in the centre of the main circle, a fallen but still recognisable altar. We gathered later from Dr Campbell that the dates during which the nunnery was occupied are completely unknown. There's no mention of it in any literary source. Its former use was simply passed down by word of mouth and confirmed by the Gaelic name of the cliffs above it, which means 'The Cliffs of the Holy Women'.

Mary Flora Steele told us later that her mother had spoken about "A cure to be had from the water that flows from the spring in the nunnery."

We got back to camp about teatime, bringing with us a decent amount of driftwood from the shore, only to discover our little valley had been completely overrun by sheep. It was evidently the spot to which all the island's sheep are driven when the lambs are to be separated from the ewes. This is what Hector and his dogs had been doing during the day, so by evening, several hundred lambs were bleating for their mothers inside the fence. Outside, several hundred ewes were bleating for their lambs. The noise levels were astonishing: the lambs bleating in the alto range, while the ewes replied in tenor or bass. The cacophony went on all evening. I feared there would be little chance of sleep, but by bedtime, we were all so accustomed to it that we slept through.

That evening, Michael and I walked across to Sanday to buy eggs from Mary Flora Steele for the morning. There was, of course, no shop on Canna, and I recall our relief on Monday when our provisions ordered in Mallaig arrived by boat. The old lady asked us in, and in her simple but spotless cottage, where she had neither running water nor electricity nor gas, and where she cooked on driftwood, she told us of her long life. Her parents had come from Barra when she was a small child. After they died, Mary Flora shared the croft with her two brothers for many, many years. Twelve months before, however, one of the brothers died. The second had just died a few weeks ago.

"So now," she said, "'tis verra, verra lonely."

But she didn't complain. In fact, according to Mary Flora, everything was "verra nice". Master Campbell was "verra nice," and so was Mistress Campbell. The party they gave every Christmas was "verra nice," and the confirmation had been "verra nice". It was "verra nice" to have the electric lamp on the causeway near the shrine, and it had been "verra nice" of us to call and have a chat. She told us how, in the old days, there were no fewer than 100 crofts on Sanday, but now, apart from her own, only two were occupied and one of those was empty since the schoolmistress was away on holiday. So, for daily company, Miss Steele had just her cat, her hens and her two cows. I shall never forget her gentle voice, her sweet face and her conviction that everything and everybody was "verra nice".

On the shore of Sanday opposite our site was a small sandy beach that invited swimming. Frank led a party there one morning, and on our last afternoon, though grey and drizzling, I felt constrained to do the same, rather for the sake of getting clean than for any pleasure that was likely to come of it. But a kind of wild pleasure ensued, with the boisterous hilarity of singing and shouting to persuade oneself that the sea is not as wild as it looks, nor the rain as wet as it feels. Seven or eight of us swam in the rain and came back to camp in high spirits. Stephen Andrews, who has a way of noticing things, found a dead seagull with a ring on its leg. Andrew and Robert explained the procedure for sending the ring to the British Trust for Ornithology, and many months later, Stephen received a letter thanking him and telling him the date and place at which the bird had been ringed.

Later that afternoon, we met a couple who had just sailed from Barra in a small rubber dinghy with an outboard engine. What's more, in the course of their voyage, they had become engaged. The voyage, rather than the engagement, seemed to us a highly risky venture, and a few locals spoke of it in yet harsher terms.

"Foolhardy...the kind of thing that causes much anxiety and trouble," said one.

Hebrideans know the sea too well to take chances with it, and they don't like to see other people taking chances either.

On our last evening, I felt that I must call on Dr Campbell to thank him for the privilege of visiting Canna. Michael came along too. We made ourselves as presentable as possible, but it was raining and the track was muddy, and though we appreciated it, we were a little embarrassed when invited into Mrs Campbell's lovely drawing room. But everyone was very kind. We talked of Dr Campbell's study of the moths and butterflies of Canna, and he gave us a copy of his paper on the subject. We chatted about the nunnery and of the Celtic cross marked on the map, which we found overgrown with nettles.

"Ah," said Mrs Campbell, "that's comparatively recent. I have some much older things in here." She took us into the dining room, and there, under the window, were a dozen or more stones inscribed with primitive designs – in most cases, including a cross. Mrs Campbell added, "We've had archaeologists to look at these, and they think they're from the sixth century."

I said to Michael, "I think we're probably looking at some of the oldest Christian antiquities in Britain."

Mrs Campbell explained where they had come from. Apparently, that Celtic cross stands in the centre of what was once the island's cemetery. In the last century, the cemetery was cleared by a strict Protestant on the island who didn't care for the 'popish' carvings on the ancient gravestones. He had them scattered, thrown down ditches or built into walls. Mrs Campbell found these treasures in such places, during her many walks. She is always on the lookout for more. I felt it had been an unusual privilege to see and hear about those ancient stones, and I shall long remember that hour spent in the lovely house among the trees. With characteristic kindness, Dr Campbell ran us back to camp in his car.

We were moving early the following morning, for the boat was due at 8am. The farmer came with his tractor and, for some reason, decided to drive, not along the 'main road' but along the ancient track that runs inland of the old cemetery. He found this was impassable and, in turning round, came within an ace of overturning the trailer. But we reached the quay in good time. There followed a chatty 20 minutes with our driver; with Dr and Mrs Campbell, who were seeing off a guest – a lady from Manhattan who dealt in rare books; and with Hector, the shepherd, who doubled up as pier master. *Lock Arkaig* soon floated in, and we were off.

Our return to Mallaig took us via Rhum and Canna. At Rhum, I recall there was a considerable delay in getting a horse aboard, and at Eigg, we were rejoined by the Expedition. Since we had been to Canna as well as Eigg, we couldn't help feeling that our holiday had been rather more of an *expedition* than theirs, especially when we learned that they hadn't even 'conquered' the Sgùrr of Eigg. As a matter of fact, we felt then like prospectors in the Canadian north-west, making for 'the big city'. Since there had been only that comical little shop on Eigg and none at all on Canna, we were, so to speak, loaded. The rest of the day, our number went on a spending spree in Mallaig, interrupted only by lunch and tea in the familiar café.

After tea, we sought out the familiar camping spot on the cliffs above the village. It seemed to have got smaller than last year, and we had some difficulty in finding room even for the bare minimum of tents. But all went well, and we were packed up and down at the station in plenty of time for the train at 7.30am the following morning. I remember wondering if it left at 7.30am or 7.35am.

When I enquired about the reason, the porter said, "Och, there's a young lady in the village who wanted to catch the train, but she's overslept."

At 7.40am, the young lady came running down the hill. She jumped on, and the train left.

It was a long, pleasant journey home. We returned, as we had set out, by the east coast route via Edinburgh and Newcastle, and I remember, during that sunny afternoon, how rich and prosperous the corn fields of the east of Britain seemed. I remember thinking how long it had been since I had seen anything of the east of Britain. For so long now, all my holidaying had been in the west. I had almost forgotten what the east is like.

York came at last, and our bus was waiting to take us on the final stage of our journey. A little before we reached Rochdale, a fine bottle of whisky was given to me as a thank you present. But it was I who should really have been saying thank you, for as usual, I had got far more out of the camp than I'd put into it. Perhaps these reminiscences of the camp may be, in part, my way of saying thank you for it.

Not that they're complete. Already, other bits and pieces have occurred to me that have been missed out from their proper place. There was, for instance, the alarm Peter Holme caused one night to Stephen and Frank by waking them at some unearthly hour and announcing, as he cowered in the corner of the tent, that he had just been swallowed by a whale. There were the lengthy discussions that went on between Michael and Frank on 19th-century English history. It took the whole of the walk up and down the Sgùrr of Eigg to deal with Canning and the Duke. There was Peter Scott's evident belief that nothing north of the border is quite real, quite normal or quite what it's supposed to be, since Scotland is full of 'sort of mountains' and 'sort of lochs' and on which 'sort of boats' may be seen 'sort of sailing'. There were Peter Holme's demonstrations of karate, and of course, Andy Holt's jokes. There was, not least, the success of our new campers – Jerry Whitsey, Philip Taylor, David Holt, Shaun Andrews and Peter Scott – in getting the hang of things, not fussing and generally fitting in. And, yes, there were many other things that I didn't notice or know of, because I didn't happen to be around when they happened. Perhaps what I've written will bring some of these other things back to mind, for once the memory is set to work, it's surprising how much it's found to contain.

# Chapter 9

So recent is our last camp in August this year, and so strong my conviction that it has proved the best of all our camps, I must ration my enthusiasm and restrain the flood of memories. I must remind myself that a good historian doesn't tell everything, but rather he selects what is significant. And the significant is that which leads to further questions, more fields for investigation or, at the humble level at which I'm writing, further personal memories.

Why did we think of the Isle of Colonsay? I believe it was because, according to the guidebooks, Canna and Colonsay are alike in being both beautiful but rarely visited. The books point out that accommodation is limited on both islands and camping rarely permitted. Few people know these two islands. They're little discussed, and their fame doesn't equal their true worth.

Last year, we had asked if we might visit Canna and had been kindly welcomed. We had loved the island, and so it was natural that, this year, we should ask if we might visit Colonsay. I wrote to Lord Strathcona explaining the nature of our party and received his ready permission, subject only to the provision that the site wasn't already promised to a similar party on 'our' dates. A few days later, to my great delight, I heard from His Lordship's agent, Major Quinn, that the site would be available for us at our requested period. The major also included helpful information about shops, water supply and transport, plus boat sailings from Oban.

It was, in fact, news to me that the boat for Colonsay sailed from Oban. I hadn't heard of the change in services and had envisaged a rather difficult journey via West Loch Tarbert and the Isle of Islay. I'd even looked into the possibility of chartering aircraft to Colonsay, but I'd rejected the idea on discovering the price. So, it was good news that we could sail from Oban at 5.30pm on Monday and arrive at Colonsay at 8pm. The news seemed better still when we found a reasonable train connection. We could set out around midnight on Sunday, be in Oban in time for lunch on Monday, have tea on the boat and get our tents up on Colonsay before nightfall. Transport was even arranged to take us from the quay at Colonsay to the site at Machrins Bay (see top photograph on page 100), some 2.5 miles away. Information from the map and from Major Quinn gave us a good idea of what the site would be like, including a large area of *machir* on the western shore of the island and water from a well called Tobar Fuar – which was marked on the map. There would also be easy access to driftwood from the shore.

It was helpful that everything arranged itself so easily, since we were a larger party than for many years and we included several young first-timers. At the other end of the scale, however, was a good weight of experience and capability – enough to ensure care of the youngsters. This hefty experience was further increased when Peter Holme found he could join us for the first few days. The others of the party included Michael Daman, Tony Layton, David Francis, Stephen Andrews, Ian Aitchison, David Whitehead, Brent Andrews, Jerry Whitsey, David Holt, Philip Taylor, Peter Scott, Shaun Andrews, Russell Howard, William Cunningham, Tommy Logan, Andrew Hall, Paul Cotton, Stephen Marsh, Richard Shepherd and Geoffrey Harwood. Of the total number of 22, eight were first-timers.

Not only were the preparations satisfactory and the party nicely balanced, but the weather had been good too, and the forecast was even better for several days ahead. So it was, with a sense that things were almost too good to be true, that I shut my door at 11.30pm on that Sunday night and joined the crowd of campers and parents assembling in the moonlight in the forecourt of the church. All who should have been present were present, including seven fathers who had agreed to run us by car and van to catch the Glasgow train at Wigan. With Mr Howard as pathfinder, they took us smoothly along the motorway and straight to the station entrance at Wigan at 1.20pm precisely. The train for the north drew in, and once our reserved compartments had been cleared of trespassers, we were on our way. The excitement of the youngsters was undiminished, even at that hour in the morning.

It didn't seem very long before, at 6am, we were in Glasgow Central Station. We made the usual transit to Glasgow Queen Street – the three tea chests in a taxi, and the other kit on our shoulders. We had to wait at Queen Street until 8.35am, but once the buffets and snack bar had opened at 7am, time passed quickly enough. The youngsters took deplorable photographs of themselves in those station kiosks while Brent ate sardines on toast. Michael, Peter and I shared what we knew of Sir Robert Peel, whose statue dominated the square outside the station buffet.

Then, precisely on time, we were off on the West Highland Line, on a morning that got ever sunnier and hotter, along the Clyde and Loch Long (where, as usual, we caught sight of a submarine). We swung north to Loch Lomond, and then through Crianlarich and Tyndrum, skirting Rannoch Moor. We then turned westwards, through Dalmally and alongside Loch Awe, which sparkled in the sun, before passing through the Pass of Brander, and then, towards noon, we dropped down into Oban.

It was hot in Oban: so hot, in fact, that we were by no means clamouring for food. It seemed wise to delay lunch until 2pm, which was to be taken in the Bayview Café, remembered from a former visit. Our lunch didn't come amiss. There was shopping for presents – somewhat premature, in my opinion – and Tony took the juniors up to McCaig's Folly, which overlooks the town. Michael and I, meanwhile, bought more provisions, and then we assembled ourselves and the kit at 4.30pm on the sun-baked quay and awaited our ship, the *Claymore*.

It was soon evident that the *Claymore* was going to be late. It didn't arrive from Coll until after 5pm, and it took some time unloading and reloading. As we waited on the quay a young man approached me and announced that he and his mate were the 'advance party' of the Public Schools Hebridean Exploration Society (he said it as though capitalised), and that they were going to camp on Colonsay. He wanted to know who we were and whether we had permission to camp on Colonsay. He wanted to know a lot of other things as well. I'm afraid he had the wrong kind of public-school confidence, and Peter said he was a good example of how not to get on with people. Another young man on the quay was easier to talk to. He was a bearded Canadian who had travelled most of the world, and now, for the first time, he was visiting the Hebrides. How he had come to pick on Colonsay as his chosen island among the Hebrides wasn't clear to me then, nor did it ever become clear, although we saw much of him later. (But of the Canadian, more later.)

Slowly, the work of unloading the *Claymore* went on. We learned that there were sheep from Coll to be unloaded – that was clearly going to take time. We carried our own kit onboard and waited on deck as those minutes turned into hours. It was pleasant enough sitting there in the warm evening sunlight, but my anxiety over our arrival time in Colonsay started to grow. It would be after dark, and although we were expecting a full moon, I wasn't sure of our ability to sort out guy lines and locate brailing pegs only by moonlight. However, there was nothing we could do about it.

Around 7pm, we found that, although there was still no sign of sailing, the restaurant was now open, and it seemed a good idea to take tea – a high tea – and it was enjoyed, since I always enjoy meals on boats. Lord and Lady Strathcona were also taking tea, and they introduced themselves to us. They suggested we might stay in the village hall overnight (why not?) and leave pitching camp until the following morning. So, what I had secretly hoped to obtain as a favour was spontaneously offered, and Colonsay's kindness was already becoming apparent. I faced the future with greater equanimity.

After tea, towards 8pm, those noises began that suggest a vessel is gathering itself for action. They include different sounds from the engine; a few sharp, though unintelligible, shouts; and sailors moving briskly, here and there. Sure enough, they presaged our departure into the evening sunshine, with the island of Kerrera on our starboard side and, to port, that stretch of the Argyll coast south of Oban, which was new to us. It was lovely on deck, with the warmth of a mellow evening and a perfectly tranquil sea. Before long, I found myself acting as a back rest and pillow for Richard, whom tiredness had, at long last, overcome. One minute, he was as lively as a cricket, and the next, he had visibly slumped. A moment later, he was fast asleep. So, I sat there for a long time, talking in a rather ungainly way to Lady Strathcona, with whom I was sitting back to back. Various colleagues came and went, chatting with us for a while. As darkness fell, the moon rose – a big, orange moon – in a cloudless sky, while a chill came on too with the night.

We carried Richard, still asleep, and Andrew Hall down below, and laid them – like a pair of corpses – on the cabin seats while I had a little visit to the bar. There, I met an American photographer who was working for *National Geographic*. He was taking pictures for an article in the magazine, which was on the Inner Hebrides and due to appear around May 1974. He was island-hopping with all the briskness that boat and air services would allow, taking in a wedding on such an island, and sheep shearing or Highland Games on another. In just a few weeks, he had travelled extensively and discovered a great deal about the Hebrides, but one island – Canna – had been outside his itinerary and his knowledge. Having been there so recently and having loved it so much, I told him all I knew about Canna, its scenery, its antiquities and its people. He made vigorous notes. When the article appears, and if it contains even one photograph of Canna, I shall feel proud to know the responsibility for it is partly mine.

Meanwhile, we were drawing near to Colonsay. Equanimity began to give way to excitement. We were nearing the end of a long journey, and what's more, the warm night – with that gorgeous moon – breathed excitement. When, at last, we drew up at the quayside, and I looked down on the crowded, animated scene, I felt caught up in an atmosphere of drama and delight. People were laughing, passengers were glad their long journey was over, the waiters on the quay were relieved that their wait had ended, and some people were shouting to make themselves heard above the engine noise while others waved and hurried about their ways. All this was happening as if on a stage in the circle of light cast by the lamps on the quay and shining from the deck and portholes of the *Claymore*. Beyond the stage, one became conscious of the moonlit world of hills and water – like watching an audience beautiful and new to us, and therefore, in itself, quite dramatic. Never before had we berthed at night in the Hebrides and this first experience, on so fair an evening, is one I shall never forget.

On the quay, Lady Strathcona helped me to identify Mr Williams, who had a tractor and trailer at our disposal, and he, in turn, pointed out our minibus and its driver. Tony's quick eyes noticed a spare trolley, and within moments, we had our kit away from the confusion at the end of the quay. Peter packed the juniors into the minibus and went on ahead with them to the hall, while the rest of us piled our kit and ourselves onto the tractor and trailer.

*"Dinnae get too near the sides,"* Mr Williams shouted. *"They're not so safe."*

We could believe it.

At the last moment, our bearded Canadian friend appeared. Could he share our camp, he asked, as he had nowhere to go? I replied that, for tonight, it wasn't going to be a camp, but rather a village hall, and he that he was welcome to share that with us. So, another body and another load of kit went onto the creaking trailer. Tony squeezed into the cab of the tractor beside Mr Williams, while I stood on the tow bar, and off we went.

It was a ride of around 3.5 miles and a memorable ride too, with the moon so bright it cast shadows all around. There were glimpses of water, glinting in the moonlight; along with hills and woods; plus hints of beautiful coast and countryside for us to explore. Mr Williams kept up an animated conversation with Tony, and his eyes seemed to be rarely on the road. But Mr Williams knew the track well – well enough to warn me, on my precarious perch, whenever we came to a sharp corner, and well enough to bring us safely to our journey's end at the Scalasaig Village Hall.

As village halls go, Scalasaig – and we have a wide experience of them – was a good one. But had it been the crudest shanty, it would have been welcome that night. The moment the kit was unloaded, sleeping bags were out and bodies were prone, silence descended, and in a few moments, I was also fast asleep.

I awoke nine hours later, still with silence in the hall. Outside, sunshine and a glorious morning greeted us on Colonsay, so everyone was up comparatively quickly. A problem arose about breakfast. The supplies we had ordered on the island – including bread, milk, butter and bacon – were still at the shop 3.5 miles away, and nothing in the tea chests was appropriate for breakfast. So a curious breakfast followed of tinned pineapple, cream crackers with Spam, and black coffee. After breakfast, Peter set off for the shop with a party to buy food for lunch, which we had back at the hall. It was going to be mid-afternoon before Mr Williams would be free with his tractor to take us the further 3.5 miles on to Machrins Bay.

For those of us still at the hall, the morning passed principally with cricket. The pitch was the road – the *main* road of the island – which ran alongside the hall. Every 10 minutes or so, the wicket had to be moved aside to allow a car or tractor to come by. On one occasion, the wicket was moved so a man could comfortably walk by. Otherwise, we were undisturbed. Peter and the others brought soup and cheese for lunch in the hall. And after that, even more cricket ensued, with proceedings enlivened by our Canadian guest. Ken brought to cricket the techniques and the panache of baseball. When he hit the ball, the results were usually unpredictable, but always impressive.

Around 4pm, Mr Williams arrived with his tractor. The seniors loaded themselves and the kit on board and set off for Machrins Bay, via the village, with the aim of collecting the remainder of our stores. The juniors and I made our way to the site on foot by the back road. In their eagerness to see the site, most of my young companions were soon way ahead of me. But Philip and Andrew Hall walked along with me, the afternoon sun beating down. We passed through woods more extensive than I had ever seen in the Hebrides and ambled beside the length of Loch Fada. For the last mile, along the winding road behind the shore, we caught our first glimpse of the site. Mr Williams then appeared, turned round and gave us a brief but welcome lift on his trailer. In a moment or two, the big stretch of *machir* came into view, more extensive than I could have imagined from the map. We rounded a bluff of rocks, and there – in the most attractive spot of all, on the edge of the beach – was the rest of our party, busy pitching tents, already getting on with the job.

Peter had planned the layout exactly as I would have done. It felt great to be surplus to requirements at a time like this, when camps are often hectic and most tiring. Most of the tents were up, a space for the fire had been allocated, and a party was out searching for wood. Michael, who had done so much in preparing and packing for camp, knew exactly where everything was. And the whole operation went with a smoothness and efficiency – no credit to me; it was extremely pleasing. A short time after, tents were allocated to their occupants, a good meal had been prepared and eaten, and most of the party were either swimming or splashing about in the sea in the golden evening sunshine.

Our tents, as I mentioned, were right on the edge of the beach. In fact, they were on what had once been the beach. Thousands of years ago, the water level around the Hebrides was higher than it is now. Raised beaches, now covered with grass, have been left at various levels, between 10 and 100 feet. We were at the 10-foot level. Below the firm – and in Michael's opinion, excessively hard – surface of the *machir*, lay several feet of equally firm sand. This made the digging of latrines and grease pits very easy, and we dug out pits of unprecedented dimensions. Within a few yards, we had a well, Tobar Fuar (in Gaelic, meaning 'Cold Well'), which appeared among a bed of watercress and trickled out through an old iron pipe. There were also plentiful supplies of driftwood among the rocks at either end of our bay.

The bay itself was about 0.5 miles across, sloping so gently that, even at high tide, the water was nowhere more than about four feet deep. A low, small island – which was accessible over the sand at low tide

– lay across its mouth. The sand itself was firm but not deep, giving way a couple of inches below the surface to grey mud, which to the satisfaction of our fishermen, especially Geoff and Ian, proved a good source of lugworms. The sand was of a less silvery hue than on Coll or South Uist. It's presumably less rich in the lime of powdered shells, and it's no doubt for this reason that the *machir* of Colonsay is less rich in flowers than on other islands.

Since we've returned, I've read an interesting tale about this beach in Loder's authoritative book on Colonsay.[16] Its Gaelic name means 'The Beach of the Battle of the Birch Sheaves'. Local tradition says a battle took place here, centuries ago, between local Celts and invading Norsemen. Although the 'birch sheaves' were apparently primitive weapons, many died in the battle, and in succeeding centuries, the bones of ancient fighters have turned up in nearby sand or mud. Since human bones lie there, it's said to be unlucky to dig for lugworms on that beach. According to the tale, anyone who does so will be punished by a storm. Well, Geoff, Ian and several others dug up plenty of lugworms, and they caused no storm – unless we owe that rain on the last morning to them! Perhaps they were let off because they acted in ignorance?

Behind our site, perhaps a mile inland from the shore, lay a half circle of hills, reminiscent of the great amphitheatre behind us on the Isle of Eigg. Although not as high or impressive as those cliffs on Eigg, they looked just as dramatic and beautiful when the moon came up. The highest, Beinn nan Caorach, was 'conquered' by most of our party. Though the peak is not much over 400 feet, it offers a magnificent view. When Michael and I walked up to the summit, we were reminded of Beinn Mhartain on the west coast of Barra.

The extent of the *machir* was huge – big enough for 1,000 tents. And so it was that, during our first few days, a second impressive array of tents, along with marquees and cooking shelters, was erected for the Hebridean Explorers by their 'advance party'. And on the Friday, the Hebridean Explorers themselves arrived. Their camp was some distance from ours, and apart from a certain amount of din at nights, they didn't disturb us much.

The surrounding *machir* was ideal for cricket, and I've never seen so much cricket played before at a camp. It was a disaster when our one hard ball was irretrievably lost among a forest of irises, down at deep long on. Peter retrieved the situation on his way home through Oban, where he posted on to us, not a cricket ball – such a thing is difficult to find in Scotland – but a hockey ball, which did just as well. The amount of cricket played would justify a long commentary on the various eccentric styles of batting and bowling on view. For example, David Francis resembled a javelin thrower in his run-up, while Richard had a most peculiar method of throwing the ball, rather than bowling. As well as cricket, we played various Canadian games introduced into camp by Ken. (I gather these lacked the subtleties and finesse of our own English game.)

Many tried their hand at fishing, and all were unsuccessful except for a complicated style executed by Ian and Geoff, which led to the pair catching three tiny plaice – too small to eat. Some wandered on the shore, collecting driftwood and shells, while others waded or swam occasionally in the lovely sea. General messing around was often the order of the day, while some of our party even enjoyed the odd conversation. I can't possibly record all the details here, since I must stick to the more distinct events that occurred when we ventured away from camp.

Wednesday was our first full day on Colonsay, and it was clear that a trip to the shop at Scalasaig was necessary, so it seemed sensible to make a mass visit to the village and picnic there at lunchtime. The walk to the village, as everyone will remember, was a good 2.5 miles, although locals often offered us lifts – especially to the oldest and youngest among us. I did walk the whole way on that first visit, and a call at the pub slaked the ensuing thirst (it was a very hot day), and then I was ready for our picnic down on the shore near the pier. I wasn't ready for what came afterwards, however. Russell started it by picking on me, so I had to put him in one of the many pools of dark, peaty water just behind the rocks. This, of course, let to retaliation, and Russell seemed to have more friends than me. Eventually, after a wild 10 minutes, most of us were either soaking wet or mud-stained. So, we decided to all jump in the sea to get clean, and we then dried off in the hot sun. It was convenient that most of us wore shorts for the entire camp. David Francis, however, was an exception. He brought a large and varied wardrobe, and then spent most of his time switching from one outfit to another.

Peter and Ken left us on Thursday evening, so they could sleep on the boat before sailing for Oban at 6am the following morning. Ken, meanwhile, had become a keen member of our camp. He came back as quickly as anyone when the whistle blew. But he was to continue his travels to Edinburgh and beyond. He promised to call in on us in Rochdale after our return home, and as some will remember, he did drop by and stayed with us for a couple of days. Peter had to return home to begin work again on the Monday. We were sorry to see him go, and no one more than I. He had been such an excellent number two. We don't make much of rank at our camps, but with more than a dozen campers, it's helpful that, in my absence, there should be one person in charge. Peter had fitted the bill admirably. When he left, I asked Michael to take Peter's place, and he followed suit admirably too. Unfortunately, as Peter was leaving, the weather started to turn, and my plan of going to the village to see him off had to be put aside. Some of the seniors went instead. Later, Peter said the part of his journey from Oban to Glasgow had been enlivened by two elderly ladies who insisted on plying him with a great deal of gin and whisky.

That threat of bad weather on the Thursday evening came to nothing. Friday brought a bright morning with an occasional shower. It seemed a suitable day to visit the Isle of Oronsay, the adjoining island, which was accessible at low tide over a sandy causeway, known as An Tràigh (The Strand). A longish walk of almost 12 miles would be involved, and I wondered how our youngest campers might manage. They did fine. First, we walked almost to the village. Tony and Ian went ahead for food supplies, and then returned to meet us at the junction for Oronsay. We had three miles to do along the road, up and down, over the shoulders of hills covered with bracken and heather. There were twists and turns, giving constant changes of direction and view. We reached the shore and saw Oronsay lying opposite, across a mile of sand. Here and there, we had to paddle a little. Richard was a little anxious about crabs, although cockles, mussels and a few oysters were The Strand's only residents. We reassured Richard that none of these fellows would bite. When we reached the rocks and shore of Oronsay, we had a brief rest among the heather and then pushed on for another mile along the track. We were heading for the one (human) feature marked on the map of Oronsay – a farm with an ancient priory beside it. We hoped there would be water there, so we could make a drink to accompany our picnic.

We sat on grass next to the priory wall, buttering bread for sandwiches with two small penknives. (The knives I had carefully put in the box had been equally carefully taken out again – presumably to save weight. I know, but won't name, the culprit.) Anyway, our sandwiches got made, and as we ate them, Stephen pointed out a layer of limpet shells in a bank near our feet. He had earlier been talking to an archaeologist on the island, who had described the middens of limpet shells that prehistoric man had left behind and could still be found today. It seemed like Stephen had found an ancient rubbish dump of his own. We began our own archaeological investigation. The limpet shells were in a layer about three inches deep. Just under the surface, we unearthed a couple of broken arrowheads and a number of stones, also broken, which had been shaped for scraping and pounding. I was sure we were handling genuine Stone Age artefacts. However, puzzlingly, there were bits of metal, along with nails corroded and marked by fire, mixed among them. It seemed illogical that Iron Age relics should be mixed with Stone Age artefacts, until someone suggested we had unearthed the rubbish dump from the previous archaeological dig – rather than one left by Stone Age man. I think this suggestion came from Michael, who was no doubt right, since it accounts for the fact that the shaped stones and arrow heads were all broken. Nevertheless, our own dig had proved absorbing. It also stimulated another dig by our juniors, further along the bank. (I've kept and brought home all the interesting bits we found.)

I had been too interested in the dig to notice that time was passing. If we were to get off Oronsay without wading, we ought to leave soon. Michael pointed this out and lured me from the bank to look around the priory. I remember David Holt and Andrew Hall were with us, and the 20 minutes that followed were even more fascinating than the previous half hour. The priory was a gem. Outside, at the west end, stood a Celtic cross, as fine as any of the famous crosses on Iona. It had a crucifix at its centre and an inscription at its foot that, even to our unpractised eyes, was almost legible. The priory roof had gone, but most of the walls were intact. We found ourselves in the cloister with two colonnades of arches, also still standing. And what strangely constructed arches they were! Here too were inscriptions – we could pick out the odd Latin word on them. We found ourselves in the church, with the walls still at their full height and the high altar still intact. Behind the altar was a recess, two feet square, with a pile of human skulls and other bones. In a niche in a wall, we found more human bones. There was, of course, no plan of the building to guide us or to interpret what we saw. There were no Ministry of Works notices and no signs to point to objects of interest. The priory had simply faded out of use, just as it had been left. It had been used for burials long after the Reformation. On one tomb, in a beautiful script, from the early 18th or late 17th century, we read this moving inscription:

*Sleep after toyle, port after stormie seas.*
*Ease after warre, death after lyfe, doth greatly please.*

It was by accident that we noticed, beside the main buildings of the priory, another building, perhaps originally a byre that had been reroofed with corrugated iron. We tried the door, and here we found, placed side by side, 20 gravestones. Three students were there, making rubbings of them. These heavily inscribed and richly ornamented gravestones included representations of what appeared to be Viking ships. Who was that grim knight whose image lay on the last stone? The students believed the stones were from the 16th century. And what I've since read in Loder[17] and Pennant[18] confirms this to be the generally accepted date. But I wonder how expertly have these stones been examined? How authoritative is that date? The style of that knight's effigy suggested, to us, a date way before the 16th century.

Our fascinating time in the priory had to be cut short since we needed to cross over The Strand before the tide came in. We managed it, and then stopped at the shore of Colonsay while we checked out a shorter cross-country route back to camp. There was no trace of a track, but the map guided us well enough over the 3.5 miles of our return hike. It was rough going though, o'er moor and fen, o'er crag and torrent, but especially o'er bog. Tony reported the following hilarious conversation between himself and Richard en route:

> Richard (indignantly): "[So and so] thinks it funny when someone falls into a bog."
>
> Tony: "Well, to tell the truth, I think it's quite funny too, Richard. Don't you?"
>
> Richard: "No, I don't!"
>
> Tony: "And why don't you think it's funny?"
>
> Richard (after giving the matter some thought): "Because I'm in the church choir."

About a mile south of our camp, we came down a steep hillside with *machir* underfoot, at the far side of which stood our tents. Some of the youngsters went on ahead and met up with some rabbits, which, strangely, didn't run off. Some of our youngsters thought the island rabbits were unusually tame, and disregarding Ian and David's advice to leave them alone, they started picking them up and stroking them. In fact, the rabbits were riddled with myxomatosis. When informed, I was horrified: not least because the youngsters might themselves catch the infection, although it has no effect on humans. But they might get that dreadful smell on their hands or clothes. It's a smell I recall with disgust from the time we came across myxomatosis on Anglesey, 20 years before. It's an appalling, lingering smell, so everyone who had touched the rabbits was ordered to touch nothing and no one until hot water was ready and they'd all had a good scrub. This was duly done, and we kept free from any trace of that smell, which I don't ever wish to encounter again.

Late that Friday evening, Jerry entertained a few of us round the fire with boiled cockles and mussels, washed down by a small quantity of Guinness. The mussels tasted, to me, exclusively of grit and vinegar. Fortunately, the darkness concealed the anatomical detail of what we were eating.

The Saturday and Sunday of our holiday were cloudy, though not cold, and were the least eventful days of our holiday. We spent Saturday morning shopping, and in the evening, we cooked four chickens by a primitive and laborious, but ultimately successful, method of wrapping them in foil and placing them at the edge of a brisk fire. On the Sunday morning, I took the simplest kind of communion service on the grass beside the tents, and then, at noon, we all attended the service of the Church of Scotland. We had already met Aldie McAllister, a member of the choir. He had made us feel very much at home and had introduced me to fellow members of his choir as 'the Dean of Rochester'. (To disclaim that title would have only caused confusion.) We had a friendly greeting, followed by a vigorous sermon from the minister, Mr Crawford, who promised to visit us later at camp. In turn, I promised to attend Mr Crawford's induction the following afternoon. As is the Scottish custom, a minister is inducted after a period of several months, during which he has been demonstrating his competence in his parish.

Sunday passed away quietly, and on Monday morning, the sun returned in all its splendour. It was a truly glorious day. We had nothing planned until evening when we were to take on the Hebridean Explorers: first at cricket, and then at football. During the morning, I found myself nicely unemployed. Michael had undertaken the shopping, while Tony's duty team had the cooking well under control. There was nothing for me to do but find a can of Guinness and a comfortable rock, and then simply ruminate in the sun. I was looking out over the beach at the distant figures casting lines or digging for worms. The sun was warm, and the quietness deep; it seemed almost too good to be true.

It was around noon when Shaun came up from the beach, doubled up with pain. The briefest of examinations in his tent disclosed the probability of appendicitis. Clearly, Shaun needed a doctor, and quickly. I knew there was a young locum doctor on the island, standing in while Dr Hall Gardiner was away. I left the finding and fetching him as quickly as possible in Tony's hands. Between them, Tony and Dr Stewart did us proud. Tony borrowed a bike from a passing girl and rode to the phone at Machrins Farm, and Dr Stewart must have set out as soon as he received the message. In no more than 10 minutes from my word to Tony, the doctor had driven to the site. The thought passed through my head that, at home in Rochdale, Shaun would probably have had to wait much longer for the arrival of a doctor.

An examination followed, and Shaun was given a tablet to ease his pain. Then came the difficult decision. Shaun's condition seemed to need urgent surgery. On the other hand, it might simply correct itself, and it would have been a great shame to cut short Shaun's camp unnecessarily. Dr Stewart said that he'd see the patient again at 5.30pm and make his decision. So, as Shaun lay in his tent, I pottered around camp while the others went off to do battle with the Hebridean Explorers.

But Dr Stewart was back by 4pm. A doctor on Colonsay must keep his eye not only on the patient, but also on the tide, since that controls access to nearby Oronsay, and it's on Oronsay – not Colonsay – that an air ambulance must land. If Shaun were to be flown out that day, a decision had to be made there and then. Shaun had to go to hospital in Glasgow.

After the decision was made, things moved fast – at least by the normal timescale of the Hebrides. The doctor drove off to telephone the mainland air ambulance crew and to summon several people attending the minister's induction ceremony whose help he'd need during such an emergency. I packed Shaun's kit and interrupted a particularly destructive spell of bowling by Michael, so as to hand over control of the camp to him. Dr Stewart returned a third time to lead a combined operation to get Shaun onto Oronsay. We drove in his little sports car as far as The Strand. There, Mrs Hall Gardiner, the island doctor's wife, met us in her Land Rover to drive us across the causeway flats, ahead of the advancing tide. Another car with another patient was waiting there too. A little island girl had injured her wrist, and since the aircraft was coming, it seemed sensible that she should also be taken to Glasgow for an X-ray. It was a total party of seven that crossed to Oronsay with no difficulty from the water at that time, but with anxiety about its depth when we'd return.

As we drove along the track on Oronsay towards the little landing strip, I caught sight of the aircraft coming low over Jura in the early evening sunshine. It was a dramatic moment to see relief for Shaun heading towards us in so impressive manner, and to feel the combination of skills and resources that were coming together to save a young life. The aircraft came directly over our heads in the Land Rover. I'll never know how the pilot landed on such an uneven, slanting patch of grass, marked only by a line of whitewashed stones, but he made a perfect landing and taxied back towards us. In no time at all, Shaun was in a nurse's care and lying as comfortably as possible on a stretcher bed in a beautiful little aircraft.

A surprising number of people appeared, as if from nowhere, around the aircraft, while the doctor wrote the necessary reports on the two patients for the hospital in Glasgow. So far, he'd had neither time nor opportunity to do this, nor had I had the chance to telephone Shaun's parents. As soon as the doctor had finished and we'd waved the plane off, there were more urgent tasks at hand. The first was to get off Oronsay, quick style. The tide had come in a long way when we reached The Strand, and the normal track was impassable. Mrs Hall Gardiner had to drive up a steep shingle bank, and at the top, she sped through a gap in the rocks that looked impossibly narrow. But her driving skills and the Land Rover's four-wheel drive got us through. We raced and splashed over a mile of mud and pools to reach the shore on Colonsay.

Mrs Hall Gardiner kindly invited me to her home to telephone Shaun's parents, but it was now about 7.15pm, and everyone in Rochdale seemed to be out. I phoned several numbers, but I couldn't get a reply. I'd have to try later. In the meantime, Dr Stewart paid his fourth visit to the camp that day to chauffeur me home.

I made my report on Shaun to my colleagues, and they, in turn, gave me a satisfactory report on their successful afternoon's work. They had defeated the Explorers decisively – both at cricket and football. We remain undefeated at camp since we lost on Islay five years earlier, in 1968.

Tea followed, and then it was a matter of setting off, once again, for the village in order to phone. Now, Tony took charge of the camp, and Michael came with me. As we padded along the 2.5-mile track in gathering darkness, I reflected that, even in an emergency, island life imposes its own rhythm. This walk, taking the best part of an hour, was part of our response to the emergency. It was, in itself, peaceful and relaxing, affording an opportunity to unwind and think.

We made our call from the pub, where there were many enquiries about Shaun and his condition. Again, everyone seemed to be out until I raised Pat Whitehead, who promised to take the message to Shaun's home. It was 10.15pm before Mrs Andrews eventually got through to me, and I was able to explain the full story. It was pleasant, then, to get a lift back to camp, even though the driver seemed to take a lot of chances on that narrow road.

Then came Tuesday and another glorious morning. It was perfect for our intended visit to Kiloran Bay (see bottom photograph on page 100), some 4.5 miles to the north-east of Machrins Bay. I had arranged for a minibus to meet us in the evening at Kiloran and drive us home, via the village to pick up supplies. But the outward journey would be a walk. And a lovely walk it was, past Loch Fada, through the woods near the village hall, and then on, passing the grounds of Colonsay House. We went through gentle dunes behind the bay, and as we came over the crest of a low *machir*-clad hill at one end of the bay, its whole length and glory lay below us.

Tony said, "This is the finest bay I've ever seen in my life," and no one could argue with that.

The beach lay there in front of us, about 0.75 miles long, with sand of rich gold, and water combining all the richest blues that one can imagine – cobalt, turquoise and ultramarine. Behind the bay, at the far end, rose Colonsay's highest peak.

While some of our party went exploring, we prepared lunch on the *machir*. We were a bit short of various things that morning, and although we shared everything with microscopic fairness, some of us were far from full by the end of the picnic. Tony and Stephen hunted the grassland for any sultanas that might have been dropped and overlooked. I even sampled the *machir* itself. The wild thyme proved pleasant, but clover flowers proved surprisingly bitter. Soon, the heat of the sun took the edge off our hunger.

I was looking forward to a little snooze, but then Andrew and Richard requested my company to search for caves at the far end of the beach. I was pleased I joined them, since they located an impressive cave with a long side passage, which stretched back more than 50 yards into the cliffs. It was eerie in there, dimly lit by a torch. The wall and roof were stained green, white and reddish brown, with lichen and chemical deposits. The imagination could all too easily weave fantastic and alarming shapes out of these colours: a reclining monster here and a hooded figure there. We were pleased with our find and showed it to Michael and another party who came along the beach a little later.

Michael, in turn, offered to show me the curious stone structure he had visited on top of Carnan Eoin, the hill rising 470 feet behind the bay. Off we went up the hill, and the next hour was probably the highlight of my time on Colonsay. We went up through bracken and heather; by a rift in the hillside, where we could hear the trickle of hidden water; and round the edge of a cliff, where eagles are believed to nest. We saw no eagles, but each time we stopped, we were offered a wider, more dramatic view of Colonsay below. We also had spectacular views of Jura to the south-east, the hills of Argyll to the east, and the entire southern coast of Mull – out to Iona – to the north. The jewel in this crown was the view of the bay at our feet: gold, blue and tranquil in the sunshine. We watched the white ribbon of gently breaking waves, which spread from each end of the bay to meet in the middle. And we spotted two tiny figures walking slowly along the water's edge. They were two from our own party, and on this glorious August afternoon, they had the whole of Kiloran Bay entirely to themselves.

Meanwhile, the stone structure on top of the hill was a puzzle. It rose about eight feet high and covered an area of about 25 square yards. It was roughly oval in shape, but with the addition of two horns or arms. It was solid from side to side and end to end – clearly not a building, but a kind of base with its stones carefully and solidly placed. Locals say the structure is associated with wartime activities of the Royal Air Force, but there's no mention of it in Loder's book on the island.[19]

We sat for a while on the hilltop, enjoying the sun and breeze, before descending once again. En route down, we paused to drink from the hidden stream, and then tramped back along the beach to join the rest of the party. Before long, the minibus had arrived, and on the way back, we picked up supplies from the village, as well as news from Mrs Hall Gardiner. Shaun had undergone his operation on Monday evening, which had been a success, and he was in a comfortable state. We then went back to camp for a big dinner, where we had the pleasure of the company of the doctor, the minister and the minister's nephew. Mrs Hall Gardiner and her son, Michael, joined us later for cocoa, when we enjoyed plenty of lively conversation about the island and its way of life. We talked about the problems the island faced, as well as its many personalities. And we discussed our own experiences during our Hebridean odysseys, as well as the minister's adventures in East Africa. The evening was filled with easy, unhurried and unpretentious talk. It was good to take part in, and it's now good to remember.

Wednesday was the last full day of our holiday. Shopping ranked high among the priorities, so we made a morning visit to Scalasaig and lunched near the pier. Michael and I had been invited to tea by Mr McAllister, so once again, we enjoyed a couple of hours of excellent conversation with Mr and Mrs McAllister, and also an elderly railwayman from Glasgow who was their guest. (We had a good tea as well.)

As we came to know the people of Colonsay, I realised that conversation with them became, for me, a major source of pleasure. The exact details of where and when all these conversations took place elude me, but I remember learning a lot from these talks. One such conversation took place in the pub with a young man who had brought his family from Birkenhead to Colonsay. He was on a deliberate quest for peace and had sought the opportunity to pursue his own personal way of meditation on Colonsay. Another woman was about to leave Colonsay to set up a craft shop on Barra. She owned a pet sheep, which had gone missing on the hills that very day. Mr McAllister talked of Kenneth McLeod, the one-time minister on Colonsay, who wrote the songs 'The Road to the Isles' and 'The Eriskay Love Lilt'. Lady Strathcona, meanwhile, told us a tall tale of the shipwreck of one of MacBrayne's vessels. On hearing the 'abandon ship' order, the crew apparently retired to the bar, leaving the passengers to launch the lifeboats themselves. The minister, on the other hand, gave us a rundown of the comical nicknames and unofficial surnames of islanders he'd known. Also, during our return sail to Oban, a knowledgeable lady gave us a number of insights on the island's archaeology. Despite their detailed knowledge, however, few people seem to be acquainted with more than one island. I'd say our knowledge of the Hebrides appears to be as extensive as anyone we met.

That Wednesday evening was a big social night on the island. There was to be a picture show at the pub, followed by a *ceilidh*, starting at 10.30pm, in the village hall. Some of the seniors went off to join in the festivities, while the rest of us spent the evening playing cricket or chatting. The minister looked in on us, and while he was with us, young Tommy Logan retired from the cricket pitch, complaining of a pain under his ribs. It wasn't appendicitis, but was puzzling all the same. Mr Crawford and I had a look at him and agreed we should, once again, call the long-suffering doctor, and so Mr Crawford went off to drag him out of the pictures. This was now not the second but the third patient from our party whom the doctor had seen. (I forgot to mention that, on the day of our visit to Kiloran Bay, David Francis had stayed back at camp with a painful foot. Jerry had stayed with him and took advantage of the doctor passing by to get a consultation for David.)

However, Dr Stewart was as kind as ever and gave Tommy some painkillers before promising to see him the following morning. And that wasn't the end of his kindness, for at about 2.30am, he was persuaded by our colleagues at the dance to run them back to camp!

Our last morning brought the only substantial rain of the entire holiday. The fire was reluctant to get going, so I scrapped it and organised cooking on a Campingaz stove in the biggest tent. Breakfast seemed to merge into lunch, although Michael found time in between them to go to the village and pay our bills. The packing went so smoothly and quickly that most of the time normally reserved for it was spent either in cricket or in making great quantities of tongue sandwiches. The rain had cleared by now, but was followed by still, heavy weather, during which the midges began to be a pest. About 7pm, David set off for the village with the juniors, while the rest of us waited for Mr Williams and his tractor. As we waited, Mrs Hall Gardiner called by. She'd heard the boat was going to be an hour late, and with typical kindness, she wanted us to know there was no hurry. The minister, with equal kindness, sent a message that the manse would be at our disposal if we wished to wait there.

Our last few minutes at Machrins Bay were spent in wandering about on the beach, dodging midges. In that grey evening, we looked back on the site, now clear of our tents and restored to its natural tranquillity. The gathering darkness seemed like a curtain falling at the end of a great play, one that would have a lasting and satisfying place in the memory.

Mr Williams arrived, and we jogged and bounced along to the village. In the pub, we had a farewell drink, and while the rest of the seniors carried on to the quay to join the juniors, Michael and I called on Mrs McAllister to take her a present of tongue, for which she had expressed a particular fondness. Once again, there was a cup of tea for us and an interesting chat, before we made our way down to the quayside. The *Claymore* was in and loading by now, and the little quay was crowded with people, many of whom we now considered friends. It was a more moving and memorable farewell than any I remember in all our years of camping.

Once aboard, we were soon organised in our various berths and cabins. At 7am, with the boat under way, we assembled for breakfast in the restaurant. A calm sea and a glorious morning made our voyage as tranquil as one could imagine. Only on the approach to Oban was there a concerning few moments when a thick sea mist came down swiftly, reducing visibility to almost nothing. The *Claymore* hove to rather suddenly, and it appeared that we had narrowly missed a fishing boat. We edged up to the pier crabwise, slowly and gingerly.

But the mist soon cleared, and Oban once more shimmered in the heat. We split up to buy presents and arranged an early lunch for 11.30am at the Bayview Café. I called the Southern General Hospital in Glasgow to see if Shaun would be fit to come home with us later in the day, and the welcome answer was that he would. So, Michael and I had then done all our duties and had 50 minutes to spare before lunch. Just at that moment, we met Dr Stewart, who had been on the *Claymore* with us, en route to Mull. He introduced us to a friend, a computer expert called Robert.

"Let us," I suggested, "use this 50 minutes rationally – 20 minutes having a coffee, and then, when the pubs open, 20 minutes having a nice, cool pint."

This suggestion met with approval: coffee in the Bayview Café and a drink in a pub round the corner. And so we enjoyed one more good conversation – all the better for being unexpected, and quite as entertaining as any of the holiday. We said goodbye to Dr Stewart with deep appreciation for all his kindness and real hope that – somewhere, someday – our paths might cross again.

At the Bayview Café, we had a brisk lunch of fish and chips, followed by ice cream. We then hurried back to the station and were homeward bound by 12.25pm. The day was as lovely, and the countryside as beautiful, as on our outward journey. (I remember particularly the colour of the rowans.) Shortly after we left Oban, there was a mass influx into my compartment. On behalf of the party, Stephen presented me with a beautiful travelling clock, along with a toothsome piece of whisky-flavoured cake. It was difficult to know what to say, apart from a simple thank you. I already felt very, very grateful for a wonderful holiday and for all the great work, humour and companionship of the whole party.

We seemed to be somewhat less broke than on previous return trips. Certainly, I was, and it was possible, therefore, to pay a brief visit to the refreshment car. With that pleasure and the great scenery of the West Highland Line, Glasgow seemed to be with us pretty soon. While Michael took charge of the move from Queen Street to Glasgow Central, I took a taxi to collect Shaun from the hospital. Within a few minutes, however, I felt like weeping over the city. I was driving through the Gorbals and passing the Govan Shipyard as the afternoon shift was leaving. There were crowds, noise and traffic all around, along with a great deal of squalor. But I was cheered up to find Shaun looking remarkably well for one who'd had his appendix removed just a few days before. In no time at all, he had finished off his tea, and we were in a taxi. Soon after, we were being greeted by the others again at Glasgow Central.

And then it was just a matter of being patient on the four-hour journey to Manchester. The same bunch of fathers waited for us there, and we split up and went our various ways.

As I wrote at the beginning of this chapter, I think that the camp on Colonsay was the most enjoyable and interesting of all the 35 camps I've been responsible for. Everyone contributed to this happy outcome, but the biggest contribution came from those six or seven whom I can hardly call boys anymore, and who have shared so many journeys and adventures in the Hebrides. In a letter to me, Dr Stewart referred to "the latest episode in the Sigma Saga". 'Saga' is a good word as it suggests a kind of tradition. Through being, as it were, the bearers and continuers of a tradition, these older campers help the younger to fit into our ways, contributing enormously, not only to efficiency but also to the good spirit of the whole proceedings. Michael pointed out that tradition not only reminds one of the past but also encourages one to see the future as the continuation of that tradition. If this philosophical reflection implies that he is hoping for further camps, I can only say that it's a hope that I profoundly share.

## Final note:

*There was one final camp after the Colonsay trip. That came two years later in August 1975, when Bill Vanstone took a group – by then, mostly university students – to the Isle of Gigha. Soon after the Gigha camp, however, Canon Vanstone's health began to deteriorate, and he retired from full-time parish work in Kirkholt in 1976. He returned, briefly, to parish life, becoming vicar of Hattersley in Tameside from 1977–1978, before moving to Chester Cathedral, where he took on the role of emeritus canon residentiary.*

# References

[1] Vanstone, WH (1977). *Love's endeavour, love's expense*. London, UK: Darton, Longman & Todd.

[2] Webster, A (1999, 11 March). Obituary: Canon Bill Vanstone. *The Independent*. Retrieved from: https://www.independent.co.uk/arts-entertainment/obituary-canon-bill-vanstone-1079750.html

[3] Tennyson, A (1833). *Ulysses*. Retrieved from: https://www.poetryfoundation.org/poems/45392/ulysses

[4] Donne, J (1632). *Hymn to God, my God, in my sickness*. Retrieved from: https://www.poetryfoundation.org/poems/44114/hymn-to-god-my-god-in-my-sickness

[5] Buchan, J (1933). *A prince of the captivity*. London, UK: Hodder & Stoughton.

[6] Keats, J (1816). *On first looking into Chapman's Homer*. Retrieved from: https://www.poetryfoundation.org/poems/44481/on-first-looking-into-chapmans-homer

[7] This quotation was not supplied with reference information in the original journal, and so it is not possible to give such information here.

[8] Pottle, FA & Bennett, CH (eds.) (1963) *Boswell's journal of a tour to the Hebrides with Samuel Johnson, LL.D 1773*. London, UK: William Heinemann. (1785).

[9] Edgar, M. (1936). *The Lion and Albert*. Retrieved from: https://allpoetry.com/The-Lion-and-Albert

[10] Pottle, FA & Bennett, CH (eds.) (1963). *Boswell's journal of a tour to the Hebrides with Samuel Johnson, LL.D 1773*. London, UK: William Heinemann. (1785).

[11] Murray, WH (1969). *The Hebrides*. London, UK: William Heinemann.

[12] Pennant, T (1776). *A tour in Scotland 1769*. London, UK: Benjamin White.

[13] Scott, W (1815). *The Lord of the Isles, a poem*. Edinburgh, UK: Archibald Constable and Co.

[14] Pennant, T (1776). *A tour in Scotland 1769*. London, UK: Benjamin White.

[15] Pennant, T (1776). *A tour in Scotland 1769*. London, UK: Benjamin White.

[16] Loder, JD (1935). *Colonsay and Oronsay in the Isles of Argyll – their history, flora, fauna and topography*. Edinburgh, UK: Oliver & Boyd.

[17] Loder, JD (1935). *Colonsay and Oronsay in the Isles of Argyll – their history, flora, fauna and topography*. Edinburgh, UK: Oliver & Boyd.

[18] Pennant, T (1776). *A tour in Scotland 1769*. London, UK: Benjamin White.

[19] Loder, JD (1935). *Colonsay and Oronsay in the Isles of Argyll – their history, flora, fauna and topography*. Edinburgh, UK: Oliver & Boyd.

# Acknowledgements

Thanks goes to Alison Harris for retyping both journals before the editing process could begin. Thanks also to fellow campers Ian Aitchison and Michael Daman, who gave early support to the project. Thanks also to Canon Vanstone's nephews, David and Richard Vanstone, who supplied interesting additional background information on 'our vicar'. And thanks to Alexa Whitten from The Book Refinery and Lindsay Corten for their patience, advice and input on the structure and layout of the book. Finally, thanks to Canon Christopher Samuels, Canon Vanstone's former curate at St Thomas' Church, Kirkholt, in the early 1970s, who encouraged me in this labour of love and of gratitude to Canon Vanstone. Chris, who spent five years as Bill's curate, also became infected by the Hebridean bug. Now aged 81, Chris has visited 79 out of a total of 120 Scottish islands in a 40-year-long period of 'crazy excursions' to the Hebrides.

# About the Author

According to his obituary in *The Independent* in March 1999, Canon Bill Vanstone was the "most intellectually brilliant of the many able men ordained after the Second World War". Despite several offers of top academic posts, Vanstone committed himself entirely to parish work in northern council estates for almost three decades. Following a heart attack and ill health in later life, Vanstone wrote a number of spiritual texts and books; for example, his *Love's Endeavour, Love's Expense: The response of being to the love of God* (1977, published by Darton, Longman and Todd) won the Collins Religious Book award in 1979.

William Hubert Vanstone was born in Mossley in 1923, in the Lancashire vicarage where his father was a Church of England vicar. After his Second World War service as a Royal Air Force pilot, Vanstone achieved two first-class degrees at Balliol, Oxford, and later, while training for the ministry, he gained a starred first at Cambridge. He attained further distinction while studying under Paul Tillich and James Muilenburg in New York. Despite his academic brilliance, Vanstone was determined to become a clergyman. In the late 1950s, he took the position of curate in charge at St Thomas' Church, Kirkholt, a new council estate in Rochdale. Subsequently, he became its vicar in 1964 – a position he held until his retirement in 1976. In 1978, he accepted the post of emeritus canon residentiary at Chester Cathedral.

As well as his published theological works, Vanstone wrote a series of journals about a number of boys' camps he led, which took place over a period of several years, mostly to the Western Isles of Scotland.

He never took holidays apart from these 'primitive camps', as he called them, to the Hebrides and other islands in his beloved west.

Vanstone was a tough, sturdy priest; he'd been a darting scrum half during his rugby days at Bradford Grammar School in the 1930s. He came to love the challenges of primitive camping, believing physical hardship and bad weather – such as those Hebridean gales that often flattened the rows of tents – led to endurance and resilience in those facing such hardships. "And when in such a place, perhaps man shows himself at his best?" he wrote in one of his camp journals. "If this is so, it's a justification – if one were needed – for camping, and especially for the *lightweight* and even *primitive* camping that has always been our custom."

Bill Vanstone – known affectionately to his young camping colleagues as 'Sir'– died in the Cotswolds town of Tetbury, Gloucestershire in March 1999.

# About the Editor

Tony Layton was born in 1956 and grew up on Kirkholt, the council estate in Rochdale where Canon Bill Vanstone worked as a local parish vicar at St Thomas' Church. Layton's first Vanstone camp, as a nine-year-old Cub Scout, was on the Isle of Arran. He subsequently attended another 12 camping tours in the Hebrides, led by Vanstone, until the last camp on the Isle of Gigha in 1975, while he was a student at the University of St Andrews. Layton subsequently trained as a journalist in Manchester before working as a foreign correspondent in Rome and, later, as an editor in Madrid. He left journalism in 1993 to establish his own company, Words&Pictures, which became a leading UK internal communications firm, winning Best UK Agency in the Institute of Internal Communications national awards in 2019. He is now a non-executive editor with the Definition Group, a public relations and communications company, based in London and Leeds. He lives with his wife, Deborah, in the village of Addingham, near Bolton Abbey in Wharfedale, Yorkshire.